The Canadian's Guide to Personal Finance

Updated Edition

by Tony Martin, BCom
and Eric Tyson, MBA

WILEY

Publisher's Acknowledgments

Authors: Tony Martin, BCom and Eric Tyson, MBA

Senior Acquisitions Editor: Tracy Boggier

Project Editor: Kezia Endsley

Technical Editor: Donald Loney

Compilation Editor: Georgette Beatty

Production Editor: Mohammed Zafar Ali

Cover Design: Wiley

Cover Image: © art-sonik/Getty Images

The Canadian's Guide to Personal Finance, Updated Edition

Published by John Wiley & Sons, Inc.
111 River St.
Hoboken, NJ 07030-5774
http://www.wiley.com

For general information on our other products and services, please contact our Business Development Department in the U.S. at 317-572-3205.

Library of Congress Control Number: 2022938391

ISBN: 978-1-119-89258-8 (pbk)

SKY10041701_012323

Table of Contents

1

Measuring Your Financial Health

How financially healthy are you? When was the last time you reviewed your overall financial situation, including analyzing your spending, savings, future goals, and insurance? If you're like most people, either you've never done this exercise or you did so too long ago.

This chapter guides you through a *financial physical* to help you detect problems with your current financial health. But don't dwell on your "problems." View them for what they are: opportunities to improve your financial situation. In fact, the more areas you can identify that stand to benefit from improvement, the greater the potential you may have to build real wealth and accomplish your financial and personal goals.

Your Credit Score and Reports

You may not know or care, but you probably have a personal credit report and a credit score. Lenders examine your credit report and score before granting you a loan or credit line. This section highlights what you need to know about your credit score and reports, including how to obtain them and how to improve them.

What your credit data includes and means

TIP A *credit report* contains information such as

- **Personal identifying information:** This includes your name, address, social insurance number, and so on.
- **Record of credit accounts:** When each account was opened, the latest balance, your payment history, and so on.
- **Bankruptcy filings:** Indicates whether you've filed bankruptcy in recent years.
- **Inquiries:** Lists who has accessed your credit report because you applied for credit.

TIP

Your *credit score,* which is not the same as your credit report, is a three-digit score based on the report. Lenders use your credit score as a predictor of your likelihood of defaulting on repaying your borrowings. As such, your credit score has a major impact on whether a lender is willing to extend you a particular loan and at what interest rate.

FICO is the leading credit score in the industry. FICO scores range from a low of 300 to a high of 850. Most scores fall in the 600s and 700s. As with university entrance examinations, higher scores are better. (In recent years, the major credit bureaus — Equifax, Experian, and TransUnion — have developed their own credit scoring systems, but many lenders still use FICO the most.)

The higher your credit score, the lower your predicted likelihood of defaulting on a loan. The *rate of credit delinquency* refers to the percentage of consumers who will become 90 days late or later in repaying a creditor within the next two years. Consumers with low credit scores have dramatically higher rates of falling behind on their loans. Thus, low credit scorers are considered much riskier borrowers, and fewer lenders are willing to offer them a given loan; those who do offer loans charge relatively high interest rates.

TIP: The median FICO score is around 720. You generally qualify for the best lending rates if your credit score is in the mid-700s or higher.

How to obtain your credit reports and score

Given the importance of your personal credit report, you may be pleased to know that federal law entitles you to receive a free copy of your credit report annually from the two main credit bureaus in Canada — Equifax and TransUnion. Equifax Canada refers to your credit report as a *credit file disclosure,* while TransUnion Canada uses the term *consumer disclosure.*

TIP: When you visit the Equifax and TransUnion websites, you won't be alone if you think you have to pay — and seemingly a lot! — to get your credit report. Even if you can find your way through the thicket of special offers, packages, and pricey subscription services, you'll be encouraged to pay for quick online access to your credit report.

However, you can obtain a credit report *for free* by using the forms each company provides and mailing them in, along with photocopies of two government-issued pieces of identification. If you're in a hurry, you can speed up the process a little by requesting reports over the phone or online. But make sure you're ordering the free report, which you can only get through the mail.

TIP: TransUnion now allows you to access your credit report online once a month for free. But before you do, remember: TransUnion is a business interested in increasing profits. No doubt the company's algorithm wizards have found that this free offering will entice more people to sign up for its paid services.

You can contact Equifax and TransUnion here:

- **Equifax:** 800-465-7166 or `www.consumer.equifax.ca/personal`
- **TransUnion:** 800-663-9980 or `www.transunion.ca` (or 877-713-3393 for residents of Quebec)

When you receive your reports, begin by examining them for possible mistakes (see the upcoming section "How to correct credit report errors" to find out how to fix problems in your reports).

You may be surprised to find that your credit reports do *not* include your credit score. The reason for this is quite simple: Although the credit agencies must provide a free credit report annually to those who request a copy, they aren't mandated to provide a credit score. So, if you want to obtain your credit score, it's going to cost you.

TIP

You can pay Equifax and TransUnion for your credit score, but we say save your money. There are cheaper ways to get your credit score. In fact, you can get your current credit score without paying anything! You can start with the FICO score estimator at `www.myfico.com/free-credit-score-range-estimator`, which provides you with an estimated range for your FICO score based on your answers to a short list of questions about your history with and use of credit.

If you do choose to pay for your current credit score from Equifax or TransUnion, be crystal clear about what you're buying. You may not realize that you're agreeing to some sort of ongoing credit monitoring service for $240 or more per year, an expenditure that generally isn't worth it. The credit bureaus' websites are clearly designed to send you down the wrong — and much more expensive — path.

How to improve your credit reports and score

Instead of simply throwing money into buying your credit scores or paying for some ongoing monitoring service to which you may not give much attention, take an interest in improving your credit standing and score. Working to boost your credit rating is especially worthwhile if you know that your credit report contains detrimental information.

Here are the most important actions that you can take to boost your attractiveness to lenders:

- **Get both of your credit reports and be sure each is accurate.** Correct errors (as explained in the next section) and be especially sure to get accounts removed from your credit report if they aren't yours.
- **Ask to have any late or missed payments that are more than seven years old removed.** Ditto for a bankruptcy that occurred more than ten years ago.
- **Pay all your bills on time.** To ensure on-time payments, sign up for automatic bill payment, a service that most companies (like phone and utility providers) offer. You can also arrange to have your credit card bill automatically paid off in full every month. Just be sure to take the time to review your statements before the payment date.
- **Be loyal if it doesn't cost you.** The older your open loan accounts are, the better your credit rating will be. Closing old accounts and opening a bunch of new ones generally lowers your credit score. But don't be loyal if it costs you!

  For example, if you can refinance your mortgage and save some money, by all means do so. The same logic applies if you're carrying credit card debt at a high interest rate and you want to transfer that balance to a lower-rate card. If your current credit card provider refuses to match a lower rate you find elsewhere, move your balance and save yourself some money (see Chapter 3 for details).

- **Limit your debt and debt accounts.** The more loans, especially consumer loans, that you hold, and the higher the balances, the lower your credit score will be.
- **Work to pay down consumer revolving debt (such as credit card debt).** Turn to Chapters 3 and 4 for suggestions.

How to correct credit report errors

If you obtain your credit report and find a blemish on it that you don't recognize as being your mistake or fault, do *not* assume that the information is correct. Credit reporting bureaus and the creditors who report credit information to these bureaus often make errors.

You hope and expect that if a credit bureau has negative and incorrect information in your credit report and you bring the mistake to its attention, it will graciously and expeditiously fix the error. But if you believe that, you're the world's greatest optimist; perhaps you also think that you won't have to wait in line to renew your passport or dispute a parking ticket.

You're going to have to fill out a form on a website, make some phone calls, or write a letter or two to fix the problems on your credit report. Here's how to correct most errors that aren't your fault:

- **When the credit problem is someone else's:** A surprising number of personal credit report glitches are the result of someone else's negative information ending up on your credit report. If the bad information on your report is completely foreign to you, contact the credit bureau (by phone or online) and explain that you need more information because you don't recognize the creditor.
- **When the creditor made a mistake:** Creditors make mistakes, too. You need to write or call the creditor to get it to correct the erroneous information that it sent to the credit bureau. Phoning the creditor first usually works best. (The credit bureau should be able to tell you how to reach the creditor if you don't know how.) If necessary, follow up with a letter or email to document and provide a record of your request.

TIP

Whether you speak with a credit bureau or an actual lender, make note of your conversations. If representatives say that they can fix the problem, get their names, email addresses, and phone extensions and follow up with them if they don't deliver as promised. If you're ensnared in bureaucratic red tape, escalate the situation by speaking with a department manager.

Tell your side of the story

With a minor credit infraction, some lenders may simply ask for an explanation. Years ago, for example, a man had a credit report blemish that was the result of his being away for several weeks and missing the payment due date for a couple of small bills. When his proposed mortgage lender saw his late payments, the lender asked for a simple written explanation.

You and a creditor may not see eye to eye on a problem, and the creditor may refuse to budge. If that's the case, credit bureaus are generally required to allow you to add a 100-word explanation to your credit file.

Sidestep credit repair firms

Online and in various publications, you may see ads for credit repair companies that claim to fix your credit report problems. In the worst cases, these firms charge outrageous amounts of money and don't come close to fulfilling their marketing hype.

If you have legitimate glitches on your credit report, credit repair firms can't make the glitches disappear. Hope springs eternal, however — some people would like to believe that their credit problems can be magically fixed and expunged.

If your credit report problems are fixable, you can fix them yourself. You don't need to pay a credit repair company big bucks to do it.

The Difference between Bad Debt and Good Debt

Why do you borrow money? Usually, you borrow money because you don't have enough to buy something you want or need — like a university or college education. A four-year university education can easily cost $30,000 to $60,000, and double that if you include residence, room and board, or renting an apartment. Most people don't have that kind of spare cash. So, borrowing money to finance part of that cost enables you to buy the education.

How about a new car? A trip to your friendly local car dealer shows you that a new set of wheels can set you back $35,000 or more. Although more people may have the money to pay for that than, say, a university education, what if you don't? Should you finance the car the way you finance the education?

The auto dealers and bankers who are eager to give you an auto loan say that you deserve and can afford to drive a nice, new car, and they tell you to borrow away (or lease, which isn't great either). You should say, "No! No! No!" Why? There's a *big* difference between borrowing for something that represents a long-term investment and borrowing for short-term consumption.

If you spend, say, $1,500 on a vacation, the money is gone. *Poof!* You may have fond memories and photos, but you have nothing of financial value to show for it. "But," you say, "vacations replenish my soul and make me more productive when I return — the vacation more than pays for itself."

This isn't to say that you shouldn't take a vacation. By all means, take one, two, three, or as many vacations and trips as you can afford every year. But the point is to take what you can afford. If you must borrow money in the form of an outstanding balance on your credit card for many months in order to take the vacation, then you can't afford it.

The definition of bad debt

The term *bad debt* refers to debt incurred for consumption, because such debt is harmful to your long-term financial health.

You'll be able to take many more vacations during your lifetime if you save the cash in advance. If you get into the habit of borrowing and paying all the associated interest for vacations, cars, clothing, and other consumer items, you'll spend more of your future income paying back the debt and interest, leaving you with less money for your other goals.

The relatively high interest rates that banks and other lenders charge for bad (consumer) debt is one of the reasons you're less able to save money when using such debt. Not only does money borrowed through credit cards, auto loans, and other types of consumer loans carry a relatively high interest rate, but it also isn't tax-deductible.

TIP

This isn't to say that you should never borrow money and that all debt is bad. Good debt, such as that used to buy real estate and small businesses, is generally available at lower interest rates than bad debt and is usually tax-deductible. If well-managed, these investments may also increase in value.

Borrowing to pay for educational expenses can also make sense. Education is generally a good long-term investment because it can increase your earning potential. And the interest on student loans is generally tax-deductible (see Chapter 5). Taking out good debt, however, should be done in proper moderation and for acquiring quality assets. (See the later section "How to assess good debt.")

Bad debt overload

Calculating how much debt you have relative to your annual income is a useful way to size up your debt load. Ignore, for now, good debt — the loans you may owe on real estate, a business, an education, and so on (see the next section). Here the focus is on bad debt, namely the higher-interest debt used to buy items that depreciate.

To calculate your bad-debt danger ratio, divide your bad debt by your annual income. For example, suppose you earn $40,000 per year. Between your credit cards and an auto loan, you have $20,000 of debt. In this case, your bad debt represents 50 percent of your annual income: $20,000 ÷ $40,000 = 0.5, or 50 percent.

The financially healthy amount of bad debt is zero. While enjoying the convenience of credit cards, *never* buy anything with your credit cards that you can't afford to pay off in full when the bill comes at the end of the month. Not everyone agrees with this idea, though. One major credit card company says — in its "educational" materials, which it "donates" to schools to teach students about supposedly sound financial management — that carrying consumer debt amounting to 10 percent to 20 percent of your annual income is just fine.

TIP

When your bad-debt danger ratio starts to push beyond 25 percent, it can spell real trouble. Such high levels of high-interest consumer debt on credit cards and auto loans grow like cancer. The growth of the debt can snowball and get out of control unless something significant intervenes. If you have consumer debt beyond 25 percent of your annual income, see Chapter 3 to find out how to get out of debt.

How much good debt is acceptable? The answer varies. The key question is: Are you able to save sufficiently to accomplish your goals? In the later section "How to Analyze Your Savings," you can figure out how much you're saving, and in Chapter 2, you'll determine how much you need to save to accomplish your goals.

TIP

Borrow money only if you're using it for long-term investments (i.e., good debt) — for purchasing things that retain and hopefully increase in value over the long term, such as an education, real estate, or your own business. Don't borrow money for consumption (bad debt) — for spending on things that decrease in value and eventually become financially worthless, such as cars, clothing, vacations, and so on.

How to assess good debt

As with good food, you can get too much of a good thing, including good debt. When you incur debt for investment purposes — to buy real estate, for a small business, even for your education — you hope to see a positive return on your invested dollars.

But some real estate investments don't work out. Some small businesses crash and burn, and some educational degrees and programs don't help in the way that some people hope they will.

There's no magic formula for determining when you have too much "good debt." In extreme cases, entrepreneurs, for example, borrow up to their eyeballs to get a business off the ground. Sometimes this works, and they end up financially rewarded, but in most cases, extreme borrowing doesn't work.

TIP Here are three important questions to ponder and discuss with your loved ones about the seemingly "good debt" you're taking on:

- Are you and your loved ones able to sleep well at night and function well during the day, free from great worry about how you're going to meet next month's expenses?
- Are the likely rewards worth the risk that the borrowing entails?
- Are you and your loved ones financially able to save what you'd like to work toward your goals (see Chapter 2)?

If you answer "no" to any of these questions, see the debt reduction strategies in Chapter 3 for more information.

The credit card float

Given what this chapter says about the vagaries of consumer debt, you may think that you must always avoid using credit cards. Besides the convenience credit cards offer, there's another benefit when they are used properly: free use of the bank's money until the time the bill is due. (Some cards offer other benefits, such as frequent-flyer miles or other rewards.) Also, purchases made on credit cards may be contested if the sellers of products or services don't stand behind what they sell.

When you make purchases on a credit card that does *not* have an outstanding balance carried over from the prior month, you typically have several weeks (known as the *grace period*) from the date of the charge to when your bill is due. This is called *playing the float*. Had you paid for this purchase by cash or debit card, you would've had to shell out your money sooner.

TIP

If you have difficulty saving money and plastic tends to break your budget, forget the float and rewards games. You're better off not using credit cards. The same applies to those who pay their bills in full but spend more because it's so easy to do so with a piece of plastic. (For information on alternatives to using credit cards, see Chapter 3.)

How to Analyze Your Savings

How much money have you truly saved in the past year? This means the amount of new money you've added to your nest egg, stash, or whatever you like to call it.

Most people don't know or have only a vague idea of the rate at which they're saving money. The answer may sober, terrify, or pleasantly surprise you. In order to calculate your savings over the past year, you need to calculate your net worth as of today *and* as of one year ago.

The amount you saved over the past year is equal to the change in your net worth over the past year — in other words, your net worth today minus your net worth from one year ago. It may be a pain to find statements showing what your investments were worth a year ago, but it's a useful exercise.

If you own your home, ignore it in the calculations. (However, you can consider the extra payments you make to pay off your mortgage principal faster as new savings.) And don't include personal property and consumer goods, such as your car, computer, clothing, and so on, with your assets.

Plug your net worth figures from both years into Step 1 of Table 1-1. If you're anticipating the exercise and you're already subtracting your net worth of a year ago from what it is today in order to determine your rate of savings, your instincts are correct, but the exercise isn't quite that simple. You need to do a few more calculations, which are detailed in Step 2 of Table 1-1. Why?

Well, counting the appreciation of the investments you've owned over the past year as savings wouldn't be fair. Suppose you bought 100 shares of a stock a year ago at $17 per share, and now the value is at $34 per share. Your investment increased in value by $1,700 during the past year. Although that may have increased your net worth and made you the envy of your friends, the $1,700 of increased value is not "savings." Instead, it represents appreciation on your investments, so you must remove this appreciation from the calculations. (Just so you know, you're not being unfairly penalized for your shrewd investments — you also get to add back the decline in value of your less-successful investments.)

Today Savings and investments	$_____	**One Year Ago** Savings and investments	$_____
– Loans and debts	$_____	– Loans and debts	$_____
= Net worth today	$_____	= Net worth one year ago	$_____
Step 2: Correcting for Changes in Value of Investments You Owned during the Year			
Net worth today			$_____
– Net worth one year ago			$_____
– Appreciation of investments (over the past year)			$_____
+ Depreciation of investments (over the past year)			$_____
= Savings rate			$_____

Table 1-1: *Your Savings Rate over the Past Year*

TIP: If all this calculating gives you a headache, you get stuck, or you just hate crunching numbers, try the intuitive, seat-of-the-pants approach: Save a regular portion of your monthly income. You can save it in a separate savings account — ideally a Tax-Free Savings Account (TFSA) or retirement plan, such as a Registered Retirement Savings Plan (RRSP).

How much do you save in a typical month? Get out the statements for accounts and plans you contribute to or save money in monthly. It doesn't matter if you're saving money in a retirement plan that you can't access — money is money.

Note: If you save, say, $200 per month for a few months, and then you spend it all on auto repairs, you're not really saving. If you contributed $5,000 to an RRSP, for example, but you depleted money that you had from long ago (in other words, money that wasn't saved during the past year), don't count the $5,000 RRSP contribution as new savings. All you've done is move the same money from one place to another, even if it's a better vehicle for your savings.

TIP: Save at least 5 to 10 percent of your annual income for longer-term financial goals such as retirement (Chapter 2 helps you to fine-tune your savings goals). If you're not saving that much, be sure to read Chapter 4 to find out how to reduce your spending and increase your savings.

How to Evaluate Your Investment Knowledge

Congratulations! If you've started from the beginning of this chapter, you've completed the hardest part of your financial physical. The check-up gets much easier from here.

Regardless of how much or how little money you have invested in banks, mutual funds, brokerage accounts, or other types of accounts and plans, you want to invest your money in the wisest way possible. Knowing the rights and wrongs of investing is vital to your long-term financial well-being. Few people have so much extra money that they can afford major or frequent investing mistakes.

Answering "yes" or "no" to the following questions can help you determine how much time you need to spend with Chapter 6, which focuses on investing. ***Note:*** The more "no" answers you reluctantly scribble, the more you need to find out about investing.

____	Do you understand the investments you currently hold?
____	Is the money that you'd need to tap in the event of a short-term emergency in an investment where the principal does not fluctuate in value?
____	Do you know what marginal income tax bracket (combined federal and provincial/territorial) you're in, and do you factor that in when choosing investments?

____ For money outside of retirement plans, do you understand how these investments produce income and gains and whether these types of investments make the most sense from the standpoint of your tax situation?

____ Do you have your money in different, diversified investments that aren't dependent on one or a few securities or one type of investment (that is, bonds, stocks, real estate, and so on)?

____ Is the money that you're going to need for a major expenditure in the next few years invested in conservative investments rather than in riskier investments such as stocks or pork bellies?

____ Is the money that you've earmarked for longer-term purposes (more than five years) invested to produce returns that are likely to stay ahead of inflation?

____ If you currently invest in or plan to invest in individual stocks, do you understand how to evaluate a stock, including reviewing the company's balance sheet, income statement, competitive position, price-to-earnings ratio versus its peer group, and so on?

____ If you work with a financial advisor, do you understand what they are recommending that you do, are you comfortable with those actions and that advisor, and is your advisor compensated in a way that minimizes potential conflicts of interest in the strategies and investments that they recommend?

TIP

Making and saving money are not guarantees of financial success; they're prerequisites. If you don't know how to choose sound investments that meet your needs, you'll likely end up throwing money away, which leads to the same result as never having earned and saved it in the first place. Worse still, you won't be able to derive any enjoyment from spending the lost money on things that you perhaps need or want. Turn to Chapter 6 to discover more about investing; otherwise, you may wind up spinning your wheels working and saving.

How to Assess Your Insurance Savvy

In this section, you deal with the prickly subject of protecting your assets and yourself with insurance. The following questions help you get started. Answer "yes" or "no" for each question.

- ____ Do you understand what's covered, the types of protection, and amounts of each insurance policy you have?
- ____ Does your current insurance protection make sense given your current financial situation (as opposed to your situation when you bought the policy)?
- ____ If you wouldn't be able to make it financially without your income, do you have adequate long-term disability insurance coverage?
- ____ If you have family members who are dependent on your continued income, do you have adequate life insurance coverage to replace your income if you die?
- ____ Do you know when it makes sense to buy insurance through fee-for-service advisors and companies that sell directly to the public (bypassing agents) and when it doesn't?
- ____ Do you carry enough liability insurance on your home, car (including umbrella/excess liability), and business to protect all your assets?

____	Have you recently (in the last year or two) shopped around for the best price on your insurance policies?
____	Do you know whether your insurance companies have good track records when it comes to paying claims and keeping customers satisfied?

That wasn't so bad, was it? If you answered "no" more than once or twice, don't feel bad — nine out of ten people make significant mistakes when buying insurance. Find your insurance salvation in Chapter 7. If you answered "yes" to all the preceding questions, you can spare yourself from Chapter 7, but keep in mind that many people need as much help in this area as they do in other aspects of personal finance.

2

Establishing and Achieving Goals

In the personal finance world, people are regularly asked what their short- and long-term personal and financial goals are. Most people report that reflecting on this question was incredibly valuable, because they hadn't considered it for a long time — if ever.

This chapter helps you dream about what you want to get out of life. Part of this task is considering your non-financial goals and how money fits into the rest of your life goals. So, before you jump into how to establish and save toward common financial goals, you have to think about making and saving money, as well as how to best fit your financial goals into the rest of your life.

Your Own Definition of Wealth

Peruse any major financial magazine, newspaper, or website, and you'll quickly see our culture's obsession with financial wealth. The more money financial executives, movie stars, or professional athletes have, the more publicity and attention they seem to get. In fact, many publications go so far as ranking those people who earn the most or have amassed the greatest wealth.

But there's surprisingly little correlation between financial wealth and emotional wealth. That's why, in your pursuit of financial wealth and security, you should always remember the emotional side. The following sections can help you gain some perspective.

What money can't buy

Recall the handful of best moments in your life. Odds are, these times don't include the time you bought a car or found a designer sweater that you liked. The old saying is true: The most enjoyable and precious things of value in your life can't be bought.

The following statement should go without saying, but it must be said, because too many people act as if it isn't so: *Money can't buy happiness*. It's tempting to think that if you could only make 20 percent more or twice as much money, you'd be happier because you'd have more money to travel, eat out, and buy that new car you've been eyeing, right? Not so. A great deal of thoughtful research suggests that little relationship exists between money and happiness.

"Wealth is like health: Although its absence can breed misery, having it is no guarantee of happiness," says psychology professor Dr. David G. Myers, who has written and researched happiness across cultures for decades. Despite myriad technological gadgets and communication devices, cheap air travel, microwaves, personal computers, voice mail, smartphones, and all the other stuff that's supposed to make life easier and more enjoyable, people aren't any happier than they were five decades ago, according to research conducted by the National Opinion Research Center. These results occur even though incomes, after being adjusted for inflation, have more than doubled during that time.

The balancing act

Believe it or not, some people save *too* much. If making and saving money are good things, then the more the better, right?

Well, take the admittedly extreme case of Anne Scheiber, who, on a modest income, started saving at a young age, allowing her money to compound in wealth-building investments such as stocks over many years. As a result, she was able to amass $20 million before she passed away at the age of 101.

Scheiber lived in a cramped studio apartment and never used her investments. She didn't even use the interest or dividends — she lived solely on her government benefits and a small pension from her employer. Scheiber was extreme in her frugality and obsessed with her savings. As reported by James Glassman in *The Washington Post*, "She had few friends . . . she was an unhappy person, totally consumed by her securities accounts and her money." Most people, probably you included, wouldn't choose to live and save the way that Scheiber did.

Even those who are saving for an ultimate goal can become consumed by their saving habits. Some people pursue higher-paying jobs and pinch pennies in order to retire early. But sometimes they make too many personal sacrifices today while chasing after some vision of their expected lives tomorrow. Others get consumed by work and then don't understand why their family and friends feel neglected — or don't even notice that they do.

Another problem with seeking to amass wealth is that tomorrow may not come. Even if all goes according to plan, will you know how to be happy when you're not working if you spend your entire life making money? More important, who will be around to share your leisure time? One of the costs of an intense career is time spent away from friends and family. You may realize your goal of retiring early, but you may be putting off too much living today in expectation of living tomorrow. As Charles, Duke of Orléans, said in 1465, "It's very well to be thrifty, but don't amass a hoard of regrets."

Of course, at the other extreme are spendthrifts who live only for today. "Shop 'til you drop" seems to be the motto of this personality type. "Why save when I might not be here tomorrow?" reasons this type of person.

The danger of this approach is that tomorrow may come after all, and most people don't want to spend all their tomorrows working for a living. The earlier neglect of saving, however, may make it necessary for you to work when you're much older. And if for some reason you can't work and you have little money to live on, much less live enjoyably, the situation can be tragic. Often, the only difference between someone who's working but who doesn't have any savings or access to credit and someone who's unhoused is a few months of unemployment.

TIP

Making and saving money are like eating food. If you don't eat enough, you may suffer. If you eat too much, the extra calories may go to waste or make you overweight. The right amount, perhaps with some extra to spare, affords you a healthy, balanced, peaceful existence. Money should be treated with respect and acknowledged for what it is — a means to an end and a precious resource that shouldn't be thoughtlessly squandered and wasted.

As Dr. David Myers says, "Satisfaction isn't so much getting what you want as wanting what you have. There are two ways to be rich: One is to have great wealth; the other is to have few wants."

TIP

Find ways to make the most of the money that does pass through your hands, and never lose sight of all that is far more important than money.

How to Prioritize Your Savings Goals

Most people have financial goals. The rest of this chapter discusses the most common financial goals and how to work toward them. See whether any of the following reflect your ambitions:

- **Owning your home:** Renting and dealing with landlords can be a financial and emotional drag, so most folks want to buy into the Canadian dream and own some real estate — the most basic of which is your own home. (Despite the slide in property prices in some regions in the late 2000s, real estate has a solid track record as a long-term investment.)

- **Making major purchases:** Most folks need to plan ahead for major purchases such as a car, living room furniture, vacations, and so on.
- **Retiring:** No, retiring doesn't imply sitting on a rocking chair watching the world go by while hoping that some long-lost friend, your son's or daughter's family, or the neighbourhood dog comes by to visit. *Retiring* is a catch-all term for discontinuing full-time work or perhaps not even working for pay at all.
- **Educating the kids:** All those diaper changes, late-night feedings, and trips to the zoo aren't enough to get your kids out of your house and into the real world as productive, self-sufficient adults. You may want to help your children get a university or college education. Unfortunately, that can cost a truckload of dough.
- **Owning your own business:** Many employees want to take on the challenges and rewards that come with being the boss. The primary reason that most people continue just to dream is that they lack the money to leave their primary jobs. Although many businesses don't require gobs of start-up cash, almost all require that you withstand a substantial reduction in your income during the early years.

Because everyone is different, you can have goals (other than those in the preceding list) that are unique to your own situation. Accomplishing such goals almost always requires saving money. As one Chinese proverb says, "Do not wait until you are thirsty to dig a well." Don't wait to save money until you're ready to accomplish a personal or financial goal.

What's most important to you

Unless you earn big bucks or have a large family inheritance to fall back on, your personal and financial desires will probably outstrip your resources. This means that you must prioritize your goals.

One of the biggest mistakes people make is rushing into a financial decision without considering what's important to them. Because many people get caught up in the responsibilities of their daily lives, they often don't have time for reflection.

TIP: The folks who accomplish their goals aren't necessarily smarter or higher-income earners than those who don't. People who identify their goals and then work toward them, which often requires changing some habits, are the ones who accomplish their goals.

Competing goals

Unless you enjoy paying higher taxes, why would you save money outside of a Registered Retirement Savings Plan (RRSP) or company pension plan, which shelters your money from taxation? The reason is that some financial goals are not easily achieved by saving in registered retirement plans. Also, such plans have caps on the amount you can contribute annually.

If you're accumulating money for a down payment on a home or to start or buy a business, for example, you'll probably need to save that money outside of a registered retirement plan. Why? Because if you withdraw funds from a registered retirement plan, you have to include that money in your income and pay tax on it. Because you're constrained by your financial resources, you need to prioritize your goals. Before funding your registered retirement plans and racking up those tax breaks, read on to consider your other goals.

Emergency Reserves

Because you don't know what the future holds, preparing for the unexpected is financially wise. Even if you're the lucky sort who sometimes finds $5 bills on street corners, you can't control the sometimes chaotic world in which we live.

Conventional wisdom says that you should have approximately six months of living expenses put away for an emergency. This particular amount may or may not be right for you, because it depends, of course, on how expensive the emergency is. Why six months, anyway? And where should you put it?

TIP How much of an emergency stash you need depends on your situation. Consider the following emergency amounts under differing circumstances:

- **Three months' living expenses:** Choose this option if you have other accounts, such as an RRSP or Tax-Free Savings Account (TFSA), or family members and close friends whom you can tap for a short-term loan. This minimalist approach makes sense when you're trying to maximize investments elsewhere (for example, in retirement plans) or when you have stable sources of income (employment or otherwise).
- **Six months' living expenses:** This amount is appropriate if you don't have other places to turn for a loan or you have some instability in your employment situation or source of income.
- **Up to one year's living expenses:** Set aside this much if your income fluctuates wildly from year to year or if your profession involves a high risk of job loss, finding another job can take you a long time, and you don't have other places to turn for a loan.

TIP If your only current source of emergency funds is a high-interest credit card, first save at least three months' worth of living expenses in an accessible account before funding a retirement plan or saving for other goals.

Savings for Buying a Home or Business

When you're starting out financially, deciding whether to save money to buy a home or to put money into a retirement plan presents a dilemma. In the long run, owning your own home is generally a wise financial move. On the other hand, saving sooner for retirement makes achieving your goals easier.

Presuming both goals are important to you, save toward buying a home *and* retiring. If you're eager to own a home, you can throw all your savings toward achieving that goal and temporarily put your retirement savings on hold. Save for both purposes simultaneously if you're not in a rush.

TIP

If you're saving for a home, it can be a good idea to save at least some of that money inside an RRSP. Why? You can generally withdraw up to $35,000 from your RRSP to buy or build a home under the Home Buyers' Plan (HBP). (Your spouse or common-law partner can also withdraw the same amount, giving you a combined $70,000 for your down payment.) Unlike regular withdrawals from an RRSP, money taken out under the HBP isn't treated as income, and you don't have to pay tax on it. (However, you do have to repay the money to your RRSP over the next 15 years.)

When saving money to start or buy a business, most people encounter the same dilemma they face when deciding to save to buy a house: If you fund your retirement plans to the exclusion of earmarking money for your small business dreams, your entrepreneurial aspirations may never become a reality. Generally, you should hedge your bets by saving money in your tax-sheltered retirement plans, as well as toward your business venture. An investment in your own small business can produce great rewards, so you may feel comfortable focusing your savings on your own business.

Kids' Educational Expenses

Wanting to provide for your children's future is perfectly natural, but doing so before you've saved adequately toward your own goals can be a major financial mistake. This concept may sound selfish, but you need to take care of *your* future first.

TIP

Take advantage of saving through your tax-sheltered retirement plans before you set aside money in a Registered Education Savings Plan (RESP) or other educational savings plan for your kids. This practice isn't selfish: Do you really want to have to leech off your kids when you're old and frail because you didn't save any money for yourself?

Big Purchases

If you want to buy a car, a canoe, or a plane ticket to Thailand, do *not* buy such things with *consumer credit* (that is, carry debt from month to month to finance the purchase on a credit card or auto loan). As explained in Chapters 1 and 3, cars, boats, vacations, and so on are consumer items, not wealth-building investments such as real estate or small businesses. A car begins to depreciate the moment you drive it off the sales lot. A plane ticket is worthless the moment you arrive back home. (Yes, your memories will be priceless, but they won't pay the bills.)

TIP

Don't deny yourself gratification; just learn how to delay it. Get into the habit of saving for your larger consumer purchases to avoid paying for them over time with high-interest consumer credit. When saving up for a consumer purchase such as a car, a TFSA is a good place to store your short-term savings.

TIP

Paying the huge cost of high-interest consumer debt can cripple your ability not only to save for long-term goals but also to make major purchases in the future. Interest on consumer debt is exorbitantly expensive — upwards of 20 percent on credit cards. When contemplating the purchase of a consumer item on credit, add up the total interest you'd end up paying on your debt and call it the price of instant gratification.

Preparation for Retirement

Many people toil away at work, dreaming about a future in which they can stop the daily commute and grind; get out from under that daily deluge of voice mails, emails, and other never-ending technological intrusions; and do what they want, when they want. People often assume that this magical day will arrive when they retire or win the lottery — whichever comes first.

The term *retire* seems to imply idleness or the end of usefulness to society. But if retirement means not having to work at a job (especially one you don't enjoy) and having financial flexibility and independence, then that sounds great.

Many folks aspire to retire sooner rather than later. But this idea has some obvious problems. First, you set yourself up for disappointment. If you want to retire by your mid-60s (when the Canada Pension Plan [CPP] or Quebec Pension Plan [QPP] normally kicks in), you need to save enough money to support yourself for 20 to 30 years, maybe longer. Two to three decades is a long time to live off your savings. You're going to need a good chunk of money — more than most people realize.

The earlier you hope to retire, the more money you need to set aside and the sooner you have to start saving — unless you plan to work part-time in retirement to earn more income.

Many people say that they do want to retire, and most say "the sooner, the better." Yet one survey found that just 36 percent of Canadians have planned or are planning for retirement. And almost one-third haven't even begun to save for retirement. When one middle-aged man, who had saved little for retirement, was asked when he would like to retire, he deadpanned, "Sometime before I die." If you're in this group (and even if you're not), determine where you stand financially regarding retirement. If you're like most working people, you need to increase your savings rate for retirement.

What you need for retirement

If you hope to someday reduce the time you spend working or cease working altogether, you'll need sufficient savings to support yourself. Many people — particularly young people and those who don't work well with numbers — underestimate the amount of money needed to retire. To figure out how much you should save per month to achieve your retirement goals, you need to crunch a few numbers. (Don't worry — this number crunching is usually easier than doing your taxes.)

Lucky for you, you don't have to start cold. Studies show how people typically spend money before and during retirement. Most people need about 70 percent to 80 percent of their preretirement income throughout retirement to maintain their standard of living. For example, if your household earns $50,000 per year before retirement, you're likely to need $35,000 to $40,000 (70 percent to 80 percent of $50,000) per year during retirement to live the way you're accustomed to living. The 70 percent to 80 percent is an average. Some people may need more simply because they have more time on their hands to spend their money. Others adjust their standard of living and live on less.

TIP So, how do you figure out what you're going to need? The following three profiles provide a rough estimate of the percentage of your preretirement income you're going to need during retirement. Pick the one that most accurately describes your situation. If you fall between two descriptions, pick a percentage in between those two.

You need 65 percent of your pre-retirement income if the following is true:

- You save a large amount (15 percent or more) of your annual earnings.
- You are a high-income earner.
- You'll own your home free of debt by the time you retire.
- You don't anticipate leading a lifestyle in retirement that reflects your current high income.

TIP: If you're an especially high-income earner who lives well beneath your means, you may be able to do just fine with even less than 65 percent. Pick an annual dollar amount or percentage of your current income that will allow the kind of retirement lifestyle you desire.

You need 75 percent of your pre-retirement income if the following is true:

- You save a reasonable amount (5 percent to 14 percent) of your annual earnings.
- You'll still have some mortgage debt or a modest rent to pay by the time you retire.
- You anticipate having a standard of living in retirement that's comparable to what you have today.

You need 85 percent of your pre-retirement income if the following is true:

- You save little or none of your annual earnings (less than 5 percent).
- You'll have a relatively significant mortgage payment or sizable rent to pay in retirement.
- You anticipate wanting or needing to maintain your current lifestyle throughout retirement.

Of course, you can use a more precise approach to figure out how much you need per year in retirement. Be forewarned, though, that using a more personalized method is far more time-consuming, and because you're making projections into an uncertain future, it may not be any more accurate than the simple method explained here. If you're data oriented, you may feel comfortable tackling this method: Figure out where you're spending your money today (see Chapter 4) and then work up some projections for your expected spending needs in retirement.

Retirement building blocks

Did you play with LEGO blocks or Tinkertoy construction sets when you were a child? You start by building a foundation on the ground, and then you build up. Before you know it, you're creating bridges, castles, and more. Although preparing financially for retirement isn't exactly like playing with blocks, the concept is the same: You need a basic foundation so your necessary retirement reserves can grow.

If you've been working steadily, you may already have a good foundation, even if you haven't been actively saving toward retirement. The following sections walk you through the probable components of your future retirement income and show you how to figure how much you should be saving to reach your retirement goals.

Government benefits

If you think that you can never retire because you don't have any money saved, we're happy to inform you that you're probably wrong. You likely have some government benefits. Although they'll likely be bare-bones, some form of various government programs should be around to provide you with some income when you retire, no matter how old you are today. The CPP, QPP, and Old Age Security (OAS) are sacred-cow political programs. Imagine what would happen to the group of politicians who voted not to pay any more benefits!

Social security programs generally don't provide enough to live on comfortably. Federal government retirement benefits are only intended to provide you with a subsistence level of retirement income for the basic necessities: food, shelter, and clothing. They're not intended to be your sole source of income. The CPP or QPP, for example, is designed to replace about a quarter of your preretirement income — but only up to a certain limit. Few people could maintain their current lifestyles without supplementing their CPP or QPP with personal savings and company retirement plans.

Here's a quick primer on these programs:

- **CPP and QPP:** The CPP is the mainstay of government benefit programs that provide retirement income to Canadians. The CPP also replaces some of the income lost when contributors become disabled, or in the event of their death. The CPP is in operation in all of Canada, except for Quebec. There, the role of the CPP is taken by the QPP.

CPP and QPP payments are made monthly and are included in your taxable income. All workers over the age of 18, including the self-employed, are required to contribute to the CPP or QPP. Two factors determine the amount of retirement pension you'll receive: the number of years you contribute to the plan and how much you contribute to the plan over the years.

- **OAS:** The OAS pension is the companion to the CPP and QPP. Like the CPP and QPP, the OAS is nowhere near big enough (nor is it intended to be) to support you in your retirement years. But like the CPP and QPP, it will likely be a helpful — if not critical — addition to your income when you retire. OAS payments typically begin at age 65.

  OAS benefits are determined each July based on your previous year's net income. The OAS pension payments and benefits are adjusted quarterly if the cost of living has risen. OAS pension payments are taxed as regular income. Unlike CPP and QPP payments, which are based on your mandatory contributions, eligibility for OAS is a function of your income level, your age, and how long you've lived in Canada.

TIP: To get a more precise handle on your CPP or QPP and OAS benefits, contact Service Canada at 800-277-9914 or go to `www.canada.ca`. Check your income and other details, because occasional errors do arise and — surprise! — they usually aren't in your favour.

Your personal savings and investment strategy

Money you're saving toward retirement can include money under the mattress as well as money in a retirement plan such as an RRSP or a Registered Pension Plan (RPP). You can also personally earmark investments that are not in registered retirement plans for your retirement.

Equity (the difference between the market value and any mortgage balances owed) in rental or investment real estate can be counted toward your retirement as well. Deciding whether to include the equity in your primary residence (your home) is trickier. If you don't want to count on using this money in retirement, don't include it when you tally your stash.

TIP: You may want to consider counting a portion of your home equity in your total assets for retirement. Some people sell their homes when they retire and move to a lower-cost area, move closer to family, or downsize their homes. And increasing numbers of older retirees are tapping their homes' equity through reverse mortgages.

Pensions

Pension plans are a benefit offered by some employers — mostly larger organizations and government agencies. Even if your current employer doesn't offer a pension, you may have earned pension benefits through a previous job.

The plans this section refers to are known as *defined-benefit plans*. With these plans, you qualify for a monthly benefit amount to be paid to you in retirement based on your years of service for a specific employer.

Although each company's plan differs, all plans calculate and pay benefits based on a formula. A typical formula may credit you with 1.5 percent of your salary for each year of service (full-time employment). For example, if you work ten years, you earn a monthly retirement benefit worth 15 percent of your monthly salary.

TIP: Pension benefits can be quite valuable. In the better plans, employers put away the equivalent of 5 percent to 10 percent of the employees' salaries to pay their future pension. This money is in addition to your salary — you never see it in your paycheque, and it isn't taxed. The employer puts this money away in its plan for your retirement.

To qualify for pension benefits, you don't have to stay with an employer long enough to receive the 25-year gold watch. Depending on your province or territory, employees must be fully *vested* (entitled to receive full benefits based on years of service upon reaching retirement age) after either two or five years of full-time service.

Defined-benefit pension plans are becoming rarer for two major reasons:

- They're costly for employers to fund and maintain. Many employees don't understand how these plans work and why they're so valuable, so companies don't get mileage out of their pension expenditures — employees don't see the money, so they don't appreciate the company's generosity.
- Many of the new jobs being generated are with smaller companies that typically don't offer these types of plans.

More employers offer plans that, instead of specifying how much you'll receive when you retire, only lay out how much you can put into the plan in your name. Known as *defined contribution plans,* these plans allow you to save toward your retirement at your own expense rather than at your employer's expense. (To encourage participation in defined contribution plans, some employers "match" a portion of their employees' contributions.) More of the burden and responsibility of investing for retirement falls on your shoulders with defined contribution plans, so understanding how these plans work is important.

TIP

Most people are ill-equipped to know how much to save and how to invest the money. The retirement planning worksheet in the next section can help you get started with figuring out the amount you need to save. (Chapter 6 talks about investing in more detail.)

How to crunch numbers for your retirement

After you've toured the components of your future retirement income, take a shot at tallying where you stand in terms of retirement preparations. Don't be afraid to do this exercise — it's not difficult, and you may find that you're not in such bad shape. You even find out how to catch up if you find that you're behind in saving for retirement.

Note: The Retirement Planning Worksheet (Table 2-1) and the Growth Multiplier (Table 2-2) assume that you're going to retire at age 66 and that your investments will produce an annual rate of return that is 4 percent higher than the rate of inflation. (For example, if inflation averages 3 percent, this table assumes that you'll earn 7 percent per year on your investments.)

Retirement Income or Needs	Amount
1. Annual retirement income needed in today's dollars (covered earlier in this chapter)	$ ________ per year
2. Annual government benefits and pensions	– $ ________ per year
3. Annual employer pension benefits (ask your benefits department); multiply by 60% if your pension won't increase with inflation during retirement	– $ ________ per year
4. Annual retirement income needed from personal savings (subtract lines 2 and 3 from line 1)	= $ ________ per year
5. Savings needed to retire at age 66 (multiply line 4 by 15)	$ ________
6. Value of current retirement savings	$ ________
7. Value of current retirement savings at retirement (multiply line 6 by Growth Multiplier in Table 2-2)	$ ________
8. Amount you still need to save (line 5 minus line 7)	$ ________
9. Amount you need to save per month (multiply line 8 by Savings Factor in Table 2-2)	$ ________ per month

Table 2-1: *Retirement Planning Worksheet*

Your Current Age	Growth Multiplier	Savings Factor
26	4.8	0.001
28	4.4	0.001
30	4.1	0.001
32	3.8	0.001
34	3.5	0.001
36	3.2	0.001
38	3	0.002
40	2.8	0.002
42	2.6	0.002
44	2.4	0.002
46	2.2	0.003
48	2	0.003
50	1.9	0.004
52	1.7	0.005
54	1.6	0.006
56	1.5	0.007
58	1.4	0.009
60	1.3	0.013
62	1.2	0.02
64	1.1	0.041

Table 2-2: *Growth Multiplier*

How to make up for lost time

If the amount you need to save per month to reach your retirement goals seems daunting, all is not lost. Winners never quit, and quitters never win. Here are some top recommendations for making up for lost time:

- **Question your spending.** You have two basic ways to boost your savings: Earn more money or cut your spending. Of course, you can (and may want or need to) do both. Most people don't spend their money nearly as thoughtfully as they earn it. See Chapter 4 for suggestions and strategies for reducing your spending.
- **Be more realistic about your retirement age.** If you extend the age at which you plan to retire, you get a double benefit: You earn and save money for more years, and you spend your nest egg over fewer years. Of course, if your job is making you crazy, this option may not be too appealing. Try to find work that makes you happy, and consider working, at least part-time, during your "early" retirement years.
- **Use your home's equity.** The prospect of tapping the cash in your home can be troubling. You're delighted not to have to mail a mortgage payment to the bank anymore. After getting together the down payment, you probably worked for many years to pay off that sucker. But what's the use of owning a house free of mortgage debt when you lack sufficient retirement reserves? All the money that's tied up in the house can be used to help increase your standard of living in retirement.

You have several ways to tap your home's equity. For example, you can sell your home and move to a lower-cost property or rent an apartment. In general, any money you make when you sell your home is not taxed. (The home must qualify as what the tax authorities call your *principal residence*. A rental property, for instance, doesn't qualify.)

Or you can take out a reverse mortgage. In a reverse mortgage, you get a monthly income cheque as you build a loan balance against the value of your home. The loan is paid when your home is finally sold.

- **Get your investments growing.** The faster the rate at which your money grows and compounds, the less you need to save each year to reach your goals. (Make sure, however, that you're not reckless; don't take huge risks in the hopes of big returns.) Earning just a few extra percentage points per year on your investments can dramatically slash the amount you need to save.

  The younger you are, the more powerful the effect of compounding interest. For example, if you're in your mid-30s and your investments appreciate 6 percent per year (rather than 4 percent) faster than the rate of inflation, the amount you need to save each month to reach your retirement goals drops by about 40 percent. (See Chapter 6 for more on investing.)

- **Turn a hobby into supplemental retirement income.** Even if you earn a living in the same career over many decades, you have skills that are portable and can be put to profitable use. Pick something you enjoy and are good at, develop a business plan, and get smart about how to market your services and wares.

  TIP: As people get busier, more specialized services are created to support their hectic lives. A demand for quality, homemade goods — and services — of all varieties also exists. Be creative. You never know — you may wind up profiled in a business publication.

- **Invest to gain tax-free and other free money.** By investing in a tax-wise fashion, you can boost the effective rate of return on your investments without taking on additional risk.

  In addition to the tax benefits you gain from funding most types of retirement plans in this chapter, some employers offer free matching money. Also, you can invest money in a TFSA. Unlike an RRSP, your contributions must be made with after-tax dollars, but when it's inside, the money can grow tax-free, and you also don't pay any tax when you withdraw money from these accounts.

  As for money outside of tax-sheltered retirement plans, if you're in a relatively high tax bracket, you may earn more by investing in tax-free investments, dividend-paying investments, and other vehicles that minimize highly taxed distributions.

- **Think about inheritances.** Although you should never count on an inheritance to support your retirement, you may inherit money someday. If you want to see what impact an inheritance has on your retirement calculations, add a conservative estimate of the amount you expect to inherit to your current total savings in Table 2-1.

3
Dealing with Debt

Accumulating *bad debt* (consumer debt) by buying things like new living room furniture or a new car that you can't afford is like living on a diet of sugar and caffeine: a quick fix with little nutritional value. Borrowing on your credit card to afford an extravagant vacation is detrimental to your long-term financial health.

Using debt to invest in your future is called *good debt* (see Chapter 1). Borrowing money to pay for an education, to buy real estate, or to invest in a small business is like eating a well-balanced and healthy diet. That's not to say that you can't get yourself into trouble when using good debt. Just as you can gorge yourself on too much good food, you can develop financial indigestion from too much good debt.

This chapter mainly helps you battle the pervasive problem of consumer debt. Getting rid of your bad debts may be even more difficult than giving up the junk foods you love. But in the long run, you'll be glad you did; you'll be financially healthier and emotionally happier. And after you get rid of your high-cost consumer debts, make sure you practice the best way to avoid future credit problems: *Don't borrow with bad debt.*

TIP

Before you decide which debt-reduction strategies make sense for you, you must consider your overall financial situation (see Chapter 1) and assess your alternatives. (Strategies for reducing your current spending — which help you free up more cash to pay down your debts — are in Chapter 4.)

How to Use Savings to Reduce Your Consumer Debt

Many people build a mental brick wall between their savings and investment accounts and their consumer debt accounts. By failing to view their finances holistically, they fall into the habit of looking at these accounts individually. The thought of putting a door in that big brick wall doesn't occur to them. This section helps you see how your savings can be used to lower your consumer debt.

Understand how you gain

If you have the savings to pay off consumer debt, like high-interest credit card and auto loans, consider doing so. (Make sure you pay off the loans with the highest interest rates first.) Sure, you diminish your savings, but you also reduce your debts. Although your savings and investments may be earning decent returns, the interest you're paying on your consumer debts is likely higher.

Paying off consumer loans on a credit card at, say, 12 percent is like finding an investment with a guaranteed return of 12 percent — *tax-free.* You would need to find an investment that yielded even more — anywhere from 16 percent to 24 percent, depending on your marginal tax rate — to net 12 percent after paying taxes on those investment returns in order to justify not paying off your 12 percent loans. The higher your tax bracket (see Chapter 5), the higher the return you need on your investments to justify keeping high-interest consumer debt.

Even if you think that you're an investing genius and you can earn more on your investments, swallow your ego and pay down your consumer debts anyway. In order to chase that higher potential return from investments, you need to take substantial risk. You *may* earn more investing in that hot stock tip or that bargain real estate, but you probably won't.

TIP

If you use your savings to pay down consumer debts, be careful to leave yourself enough of an emergency cushion. (Chapter 2 tells you how to determine what size emergency reserve you should have.) You want to be in a position to withstand an unexpected large expense or temporary loss of income. On the other hand, if you use savings to pay down credit card debt, you can run your credit card balances back up in a financial pinch (unless your card gets cancelled), or you can turn to a family member or wealthy friend for a low-interest loan.

Find the funds to pay down consumer debts

TIP

Have you ever reached into the pocket of an old jacket and found a rolled-up $20 bill you forgot you had? Stumbling across some forgotten funds is always a pleasant experience. But before you root through all your closets in search of stray cash to help you pay down that nagging credit card debt, check out some of these financial jacket pockets you may have overlooked:

- **Borrow against your cash-value life insurance policy.** If you did business with an insurance agent, they probably sold you a cash-value policy because it pays high commissions to insurance agents. Or perhaps your parents bought one of these policies for you when you were a child. Borrow against the cash value to pay down your debts. (*Note:* You may want to consider discontinuing your cash-value policy altogether and simply withdraw the cash balance.)

- **Sell investments held outside of registered retirement plans.** Maybe you have some shares of stock or a Canada Savings Bond gathering dust in your safe-deposit box. Consider cashing in these investments to pay down your consumer loans. Just be sure to consider the tax consequences of selling these investments. If possible, sell investments that won't generate a big tax bill.
- **Tap the equity in your home.** If you're a homeowner, you may be able to tap into your home's *equity,* which is the difference between the property's market value and the outstanding loan balance. You can generally borrow against real estate at a lower interest rate. However, you must take care to ensure that you don't over-borrow on your home and risk losing it to your lender.
- **Lean on family.** They know you, love you, realize your shortcomings, and probably won't be as cold-hearted as some bankers. Money borrowed from family members can have strings attached, of course. Treating the obligation seriously is important. To avoid misunderstandings, write up a simple agreement listing the terms and

conditions of the loan. Unless your family members are the worst bankers you know, you'll probably get a fair interest rate, and your family will have the satisfaction of helping you out. Just don't forget to pay them back.

How to Decrease Debt When You Lack Savings

If you lack savings to throw at your consumer debts, not surprisingly, you have some work to do. If you're currently spending all your income (and more!), you need to figure out how you can decrease your spending (see Chapter 4 for lots of great ideas) and/or increase your income. In the meantime, you need to slow the growth of your debt.

Reduce your credit card's interest rate

TIP

Different credit cards charge different interest rates. So why pay 14 percent, 16 percent, 18 percent, or more, when you can pay less? The credit card business is highly competitive. Until you get your debt paid off, slow the growth of your debt by reducing the interest rate you're paying. Here are some sound ways to do that:

- **Apply for a lower-interest credit card.** If you're earning a decent income, you're not too burdened with debt, and you have a clean credit record, qualifying for lower-rate cards is relatively painless. Some persistence (and cleanup work) may be required if you have income and debt problems or nicks in your credit report. After you're approved for a new, lower-interest card, you can simply transfer your outstanding balance from your higher-interest card.
- **Inform the bank that issued your current high-interest credit card that you want to cancel your card because you found a competitor that offers no annual fee and a lower interest rate.** Your bank may choose to match the terms of the "competitor" rather than lose you as a customer. But be careful with this strategy and consider just paying off or transferring the balance. Cancelling the credit card, especially if it's one you've had for a number of years, may lower your credit score in the short term.
- **While you're paying down your credit card balances, stop making new charges on cards that have outstanding balances.** Many people don't realize that interest starts to accumulate *immediately* when they carry a balance. You have no *grace period* (the 20 or so days you normally have to pay your balance in full without incurring interest charges) if you carry a credit card balance from month to month.

Understand all credit card terms and conditions

Avoid getting lured into applying for a credit card that hypes an extremely low interest rate. One such card advertised a 1.9 percent rate, but you had to dig into the fine print for the rest of the story.

First, any card that offers such a low interest rate will honour that rate only for a short period of time — in this case, six months. After six months, the interest rate skyrocketed to nearly 15 percent.

But wait, there's more: Make just one late payment or exceed your credit limit, and the company raises your interest rate to 19.8 percent (or even 24 percent, 29 percent, or more) and slaps you with a $29 fee — $39 thereafter. If you want a cash advance on your card, you get socked with a fee equal to 3 percent of the amount advanced. (Some banks have even advertised 0 percent interest rates — although that rate generally has applied only to balances transferred from another card, and such cards have been subject to all the other vagaries discussed in this section.)

This isn't to say that everyone should avoid this type of card. Such a card may make sense for you if you want to transfer an outstanding balance and then pay off that balance within a matter of months and cancel the card to avoid getting socked with the card's high fees.

If you hunt around for a low-interest credit card, be sure to carefully read all the terms and conditions. Start by reviewing the uniform rates and terms disclosure, which details the myriad fees and conditions (especially how much your interest rate can increase for missed or late payments). Also, be sure you understand how the future interest rate is determined on cards that charge variable interest rates.

Cut up your credit cards

If you have a tendency to live beyond your means by buying on credit, get rid of the culprit — the credit card (and other consumer credit). To kick the habit, a smoker needs to toss *all* the cigarettes, and an alcoholic needs to get rid of *all* the booze. Cut up *all* your credit cards and call the card issuers to cancel your accounts. And when you buy consumer items such as cars and furniture, do not apply for credit.

The world worked fine back in the years B.C. (Before Credit). Think about it: Just a couple of generations ago, credit cards didn't exist. People paid with cash and cheques — imagine that. You *can* function without buying anything on a credit card. In certain cases, you may need a card as collateral — such as when renting a car. When you bring back the rental car, however, you can pay with cash or with a debit card. Leave the card at home in the back of your sock drawer or freezer and pull (or thaw) it out only for the occasional car rental.

If you can trust yourself, keep a separate credit card *only* for new purchases that you know you can absolutely pay in full each month. No one needs three, five, or ten credit cards. You can live with just one, given the wide acceptance of most cards.

Retailers such as department stores and gas stations just love to issue cards. Not only do these cards charge outrageously high interest rates, but they're also not widely accepted like Visa and MasterCard. Virtually all retailers accept Visa and MasterCard. More credit lines mean more temptation to spend what you can't afford.

TIP

If you decide to keep one widely accepted credit card instead of getting rid of them all, be careful. You may be tempted to let debt accumulate and roll over for a month or two, starting up the whole horrible process of running up your consumer debt again. Consider making all your purchases on a debit card, only using your credit card when a debit card isn't accepted.

Debit cards: The best of both worlds

Credit cards are the main reason today's consumers are buying more than they can afford. Logic says that one way you can keep your spending in check is to stop using your credit cards. But in a society that's used to the widely accepted Visa and MasterCard plastic for purchases, changing habits is hard.

Debit cards truly offer the best of both worlds. The beauty of the debit card is that it offers you the convenience of making purchases with a piece of plastic without the temptation or ability to run up credit card debt. Debit cards keep you from spending money you don't have and help you live within your means.

The big difference between debit cards and credit cards is that debit card purchase amounts are deducted electronically from your chequing account the moment your purchase is approved.

TIP: If you switch to a debit card and you keep your chequing account balance low and don't ordinarily balance your chequebook, you may need to start balancing it. Otherwise, you may face charges for overdrawing your account.

Here are some other differences between debit and credit cards:

- If you pay your credit card bill in full and on time each month, your credit card gives you free use of the money you owe until it's time to pay the bill. Debit cards take the money out of your account essentially immediately.
- Credit cards make it easier for you to dispute charges for problematic merchandise through the issuing bank. Most banks allow you to dispute charges for up to 60 days after purchase and may credit the disputed amount to your account pending resolution. Most debit cards offer a much shorter window, typically less than one week, for making disputes.

How to Stop the Spending/ Debt Cycle

Regardless of how you deal with paying off your debt, you're in real danger of falling back into old habits. Backsliding happens not only to people who file bankruptcy but also to those who use savings or home equity to eliminate their debt. This section speaks to that risk and tells you what to do about it.

Resist the credit temptation

Getting out of debt can be challenging, but you can do it with this book by your side. In addition to the ideas discussed earlier in this chapter (such as eliminating all your credit cards and getting a debit card), the following list provides some additional tactics you can use to limit the influence credit cards hold over your life. (If you're concerned about the impact that any of these tactics may have on your credit rating, turn to Chapter 1.)

- **Reduce your credit limit.** If you choose not to get rid of all your credit cards or get a debit card, be sure to keep a lid on your credit card's *credit limit* (the maximum balance allowed on your card). You don't have to accept the increase just because your bank keeps raising your credit limit to reward you for being such a profitable customer. Call your credit card's toll-free number and lower your credit limit to a comfortable level.
- **Replace your credit card with a charge card.** A *charge card* (such as the American Express card) requires you to pay your balance in full each billing period. You have no credit line or interest charges. Of course, spending more than you can afford to pay when the bill comes due is possible. But you'll be much less likely to overspend if you know you have to pay in full every month.

- **Never buy anything on credit that depreciates.** Meals out, cars, clothing, and shoes all depreciate. Don't buy these things on credit. Borrow money only for sound investments — education, real estate, or your own business, for example.
- **Think in terms of total cost.** Everything sounds cheaper in terms of monthly payments — that's how salespeople entice you into buying things you can't afford. Take a calculator along, if necessary, to tally up the sticker price, interest charges, and upkeep. The total cost will scare you. *It should.*
- **Stop the junk mail avalanche.** Look at your daily mail — half of it is probably solicitations and catalogues. You can save some trees and time sorting junk mail by removing yourself from most mailing lists.

To remove your name from mailing lists, register with the Canadian Marketing Association's Do Not Contact service. Call 416-391-2362 or go to `www.the-cma.org`.

- **Stop telemarketing calls.** To reduce unwanted telemarketing calls, register your phone number with Canada's National Do Not Call List operated by the Canadian government. For more information, call 866-580-3625 or go to `www.lnnte-dncl.gc.ca`.

- **Limit what you can spend.** Go shopping with a small amount of cash and no plastic or cheques. That way, you can spend only what little cash you have with you.

Identify and treat a compulsion

No matter how hard they try to break the habit, some people become addicted to spending and accumulating debt. It becomes a chronic problem that starts to interfere with other aspects of their lives and can lead to problems at work and with family and friends.

Debtors Anonymous (DA) is a non-profit organization that provides support (primarily through group meetings) to peoplc trying to break their debt accumulation and spending habits. DA is modeled after the 12-step Alcoholics Anonymous (AA) program.

Like AA, DA works with people from all walks of life and socioeconomic backgrounds. You can find people who are financially on the edge, $100,000-plus income earners, and everybody in between at DA meetings. Even former millionaires join the program.

DA has a simple questionnaire that helps determine whether you're a problem debtor. If you answer "yes" to at least 8 of the following 15 questions, you have a compulsive spending and debt accumulation habit:

- Are your debts making your home life unhappy?
- Does the pressure of your debts distract you from your daily work?
- Are your debts affecting your reputation?
- Do your debts cause you to think less of yourself?
- Have you ever given false information in order to obtain credit?
- Have you ever made unrealistic promises to your creditors?
- Does the pressure of your debts make you careless when it comes to the welfare of your family?
- Do you ever fear that your employer, family, or friends will learn the extent of your total indebtedness?
- When faced with a difficult financial situation, does the prospect of borrowing give you an inordinate feeling of relief?
- Does the pressure of your debts cause you to have difficulty sleeping?
- Has the pressure of your debts ever caused you to consider getting drunk?

- Have you ever borrowed money without giving adequate consideration to the rate of interest you're required to pay?
- Do you usually expect a negative response when you're subject to a credit investigation?
- Have you ever developed a strict regimen for paying off your debts, only to break it under pressure?
- Do you justify your debts by telling yourself that you are superior to the "other" people, and when you get your "break," you'll be out of debt?

TIP

To find a DA support group in your area, call 781-453-2743 or go to `www.debtorsanonymous.org`.

4

Reducing Your Spending

Telling people how and where to spend their money is a risky undertaking, because most people like to spend money and hate to be told what to do. So, this chapter details numerous strategies that have worked for other people. The final decision for what to cut rests solely on you. Only you can decide what's important to you and what's dispensable. (Should you cut out your weekly poker games or cut back on your growing designer shoe collection?)

With these recommendations, it's assumed that you value your time. Therefore, you're not told to scrimp and save by doing things like cutting open a tube of toothpaste so that you can use every last bit of it. And you're not told to ask your spouse to do your ironing to reduce your dry-cleaning bills.

The fact that you're busy all the time may be part of the reason you spend money as you do. So, the recommendations in this chapter focus on methods that produce significant savings but don't involve a lot of time. In other words, these strategies provide bang for the buck.

How to Analyze Your Spending

Brushing your teeth, eating a diverse diet including plenty of fruits and vegetables, and exercising regularly are good habits. Spending less than you earn and saving enough to meet your future financial objectives are the financial equivalents of these habits.

Despite having relatively high incomes compared with the rest of the world, some Canadians have a hard time saving a good percentage of their incomes. Why? Often it's because they spend too much — sometimes far more than necessary.

TIP

The first step to saving more of the income that you work so hard for is to figure out where that income typically gets spent. The spending analysis in this section helps you determine where your cash is flowing. Do the spending analysis if any of the following applies to you:

- You aren't saving enough money to meet your financial goals. (If you're not sure whether this is the case, see Chapter 2.)
- You feel as though your spending is out of control, or you don't really know where all your income goes.
- You're anticipating a significant life change (for example, getting married, leaving your job to start a business, having children, retiring, and so on).

If you're already a good saver, you may not need to complete the spending analysis. After you save enough to accomplish your goals, you don't need to continually track your spending. You've already established the good habit — saving. Tracking exactly where you spend your money month after month is *not* the good habit. (You may still benefit from perusing the smarter spending recommendations later in this chapter.)

The immediate goal of a spending analysis is to figure out where you typically spend your money. The long-range goal is to establish a good habit: maintaining a regular, automatic saving routine.

Notice the first four letters in the word *analysis.* Knowing where your money is going each month is useful, and making changes in your spending behaviour and cutting out the fat so you can save more money and meet your financial goals is terrific. However, you may make yourself and those around you miserable if you're completely uptight about documenting precisely where you spend every single dollar and cent.

TIP Saving what you need to achieve your goals is what matters most.

Track your spending the low-tech way

Analyzing your spending is a little bit like being a detective. Your goal is to reconstruct the spending. You probably have some major clues at your fingertips or somewhere on the desk or computer where you handle your finances.

TIP Unless you keep meticulous records that detail every dollar you spend, you won't have perfect information. Don't sweat it. A number of sources can enable you to detail where you've been spending your money. To get started, get out or access the following:

- Recent pay stubs
- Tax returns
- Online banking/bill payment records
- Log of cheques paid and monthly debit card transactions
- Credit card bills

Ideally, you want to assemble the information needed to track 12 months of spending. But if your spending patterns don't fluctuate greatly from month to month (or you won't complete the exercise if it means compiling a year's worth of data), you can reduce your data gathering to one six-month period, or to every second or third month for the past year. If you take a major vacation or spend a large amount on gifts during certain months of the year, make sure that you include these months in your analysis. Also, account for insurance or other financial payments that you may choose not to pay monthly and instead pay quarterly, semi-annually, or annually.

Purchases made with cash are the hardest to track because they don't leave a paper trail. Over the course of a week or perhaps even a month, you *could* keep a record of everything you buy with cash. Tracking cash can be an enlightening exercise, but it can also be tedious (see the next section). If you lack the time and patience, you can try *estimating*. Think about a typical week or month — how often do you buy things with cash? For example, if you eat lunch out four days a week, paying around $8 per meal, that's about $130 per month. You may also want to try adding up all the cash withdrawals from your chequing account statement and then working backward to try to remember where you spent the cash.

Separate your expenditures into as many useful and detailed categories as possible. Table 4-1 gives you a suggested format; you can tailor it to fit your needs. Keep in mind that if you lump too much of your spending into broad, meaningless categories like "Other," you'll end up right back where you started — wondering where all the money went.

Note: When completing the tax section in Table 4-1, report the total tax you paid for the year as tabulated on your annual income tax return. Then take the total Canada Pension Plan (CPP) or Quebec Pension Plan (QPP) and Employment Insurance (EI) deductions paid from your end-of-year tax slips rather than the tax withheld or paid during the year.

Category	Monthly Average ($)	Percent of Total Gross Income (%)
Income taxes		________
Federal	________	
Provincial	________	
CPP or QPP	________	
EI premiums	________	
Housing		________
Rent	________	
Mortgage	________	
Property taxes	________	
Gas, electric, oil	________	
Water, garbage	________	
Phones	________	
Cable TV and Internet	________	

Category	Monthly Average ($)	Percent of Total Gross Income (%)
Gardener, housekeeper	________	
Furniture, appliances	________	
Maintenance, repairs	________	
Food		________
Supermarket	________	
Restaurants and takeout	________	
Transportation		________
Gasoline	________	
Maintenance, repairs	________	
Provincial registration fees	________	
Tolls and parking	________	
Bus or subway fares or passes	________	
Style		________
Clothing	________	
Shoes	________	
Jewellery (watches, earrings)	________	
Dry cleaning	________	
Debt repayments (excluding mortgage)		________
Credit cards	________	
Auto loans	________	
Student loans	________	
Other	________	
Fun stuff		________

Category	Monthly Average ($)	Percent of Total Gross Income (%)
Entertainment (movies, concerts)	______	
Vacation and travel	______	
Gifts	______	
Hobbies	______	
Subscriptions, memberships	______	
Pets	______	
Other	______	
Personal care		______
Haircuts	______	
Health club or gym membership	______	
Makeup	______	
Other	______	
Personal business		______
Accountant, lawyer, financial advisor	______	
Other	______	
Healthcare		______
Physicians and hospitals	______	
Drugs	______	
Dental and vision	______	
Therapy	______	
Insurance		______

Category	Monthly Average ($)	Percent of Total Gross Income (%)
Homeowner's or renter's	________	
Auto	________	
Health	________	
Life	________	
Disability	________	
Long-term care	________	
Umbrella liability	________	
Education		________
Tuition	________	
Books	________	
Supplies	________	
Housing costs (room and board)	________	
Living expenses	________	
Children		________
Daycare	________	
Toys	________	
Activities	________	
Child support	________	
Charitable donations	________	________
Other		________
________	________	
________	________	
________	________	

Table 4-1: *Detailing Your Spending*

Track your spending on "free" websites and apps

Software programs and websites can assist you with paying bills and tracking your spending. The main advantage of using software or websites is that you can continually track your spending as long as you keep entering the information. Software packages and websites can even help speed up the cheque-writing process (after you figure out how to use them, which isn't always an easy thing to do).

But you don't need a computer and fancy software to pay your bills and figure out where you're spending money. Many people stop entering data after a few months. If tracking your spending is what you're after, you need to enter information from the bills you pay by cheque and the expenses you pay by credit card and cash. Like home exercise equipment and exotic kitchen appliances, such software often ends up in the consumer graveyard.

Plenty of folks have trouble saving money and reducing their spending. So, it's no surprise that in the increasingly crowded universe of free websites, plenty are devoted to supposedly helping you to reduce your spending.

More of these sites keep springing up, but among those you may have heard of and stumbled upon are BudgetTracker, Geezeo, Mint, and Wally. The biggest problem with these "free" sites is that they're loaded with advertising and/or have *affiliate relationships* with companies. This simply means that the site gets paid if you click a link to one of its recommended service providers and buy what they're selling.

This compensation, of course, creates an enormous conflict of interest and thoroughly taints any recommendation made by "free" sites that profit from affiliate referrals. For starters, they have no incentive or reason to recommend companies that won't pay them an affiliate fee. And, there's little — if any — screening of companies for quality, service level, and other criteria important to you as a consumer.

TIP

Also, be forewarned that after registering you as a site user, the first thing most of these sites want you to do is connect directly to your financial institutions (banks, brokerages, investment companies) and download your investment account and spending data. If your intuition tells you this may not be a good idea, trust your instincts. Yes, there are security concerns, but they pale in comparison to privacy concerns and apprehension about the endless pitching to you of products and services.

Another problem with these websites is the incredibly simplistic calculators that they have. One that purports to help with retirement planning doesn't allow users to choose a retirement age younger than 62 and has no provisions for part-time work. When it asks about your assets, it makes no distinction between equity in your home and financial assets (stocks, bonds, mutual funds, and so on). Finally, these sites generally offer no phone support, so if you encounter a problem using them, you're relegated to ping-ponging emails in the hope of getting your questions answered.

Many "free" financial websites were singing the praises of the software You Need a Budget (YNAB). It's a decent, but not exceptional, product. So what explains all the "free" publicity? The makers of YNAB pay a whopping 35 percent commission to website affiliates that pitch to users and direct them to buy the product. This means a website that promotes YNAB earns about $21 for each customer it refers to YNAB who coughs up the $60 the software sells for. Does that taint a site's recommendation of YNAB? Of course it does!

Paper, pencil, and a calculator can work just fine for tracking your spending.

The Keys to Successful Spending

For most people, spending money is a whole lot easier and more fun than earning it. You don't have to stop having fun and turn into a penny-pinching, stay-at-home miser. Of course, you can spend money. But there's a world of difference between spending money carelessly and spending money *wisely*.

If you spend too much and spend unwisely, you put pressure on your income and your future need to continue working. Savings dwindle, debts may accumulate, and you can't achieve your financial (and perhaps personal) goals.

If you dive into details too quickly, you may miss the big picture. So, before you jump into the specific areas where you may be able to trim your budget, here are four overall keys to successful spending:

- Living within your means
- Looking for the best values
- Cutting excess spending
- Shunning consumer credit

These four principles form the basis of the recommendations in this chapter.

Live within your means

Spending too much is a *relative* problem. Two people can each spend $40,000 per year (including their taxes) yet still have drastically different financial circumstances. How? Suppose that one of them earns $50,000 annually, while the other earns $35,000. The $50,000 earner saves $10,000 each year. The $35,000 earner, on the other hand, accumulates $5,000 of new debt (or spends that amount from prior savings). So, spend within your means. If you do nothing else in this chapter, be sure to do this.

Don't let the spending habits of others dictate yours. Certain people — and you know who they are — bring out the big spender in you. Do something else with them besides shopping and spending. If you can't find any other activity to share with them, try shopping with limited cash and no credit cards. That way, you can't overspend on impulse.

How much you can safely spend while working toward your financial goals depends on what your goals are and where you are financially. Save first for your goals, and then live on what's left over. Chapter 2 helps you figure out how much you should be saving and what you can afford to spend while still accomplishing your financial goals.

Look for the best values

You can find high quality and low cost in the same product. Conversely, paying a high price is no guarantee that you're getting high quality. Cars are a good example. Whether you're buying a subcompact, a sports car, or a luxury four-door sedan, some cars are more fuel efficient and cheaper to maintain than rivals that carry the same sticker price.

When you evaluate the cost of a product or service, think in terms of total, long-term costs. Suppose that you're comparing the purchase of two used cars: the Solid Sedan, which costs $11,995, and the Clunker Convertible, which weighs in at $9,995. On the surface, the convertible appears to be cheaper. However, the price that you pay for a car is but a small portion of what that car ultimately costs you. If the convertible is costly to operate, maintain, and insure over the years, it could end up costing you much more than the sedan would (later in this chapter, you find out where to find such information). Sometimes, paying a reasonable amount more up front for a higher-quality product or service ends up saving you money in the long run.

TIP

People who sell particular products and services may initially appear to have your best interests at heart when they steer you toward something that isn't costly. However, you may be in for a rude awakening when you discover the ongoing service, maintenance, and other fees you face in the years ahead. Salespeople are generally trained to pitch you a lower-cost product if you indicate that's what you're after.

Don't waste money on brand names

TIP

You don't want to compromise on quality, especially in the areas where quality is important to you. But you also don't want to be duped into believing that brand-name products are better or worth a substantially higher price. Be suspicious of companies that spend gobs on image-oriented advertising. Why? Because heavy advertising costs many dollars, and as a consumer of those companies' products and services, you pay for all that advertising.

All successful companies advertise their products. Advertising is cost-effective *and* good business (if it brings in enough new business). But you need to consider the products and services and the claims that companies make. In grocery stores, for example, you can often find name brands and store brands for the same product sitting in proximity to one another. Upon reading the label, you can see that the products may, in fact, be identical, and the only difference between the two products is that the brand-name product costs more (because of the branding and associated advertising and marketing).

Branding is used in many fields to sell overpriced, mediocre products and services to consumers. Does a cola beverage really taste better if it's "the real thing" or "the choice of a new generation"?

Now, if you can't live without your Coca-Cola or Pepsi, and you think that these products are head and shoulders above the rest, drink them to your heart's content. But question the importance of the name and image of the products you buy. Companies spend a lot of money creating and cultivating an image, which has zero impact on how their products taste or perform.

Tread carefully online

Online shopping has grown in popularity for some good reasons. It's reasonably fast and convenient, and you can quickly research different products and services before buying.

Without much time or effort, you can quickly determine what a competitive price is for a product and get it ordered and delivered in short order. No need to get in your car and waste gasoline and have to navigate traffic, possible accidents, and salespeople.

If this all sounds too good to be true, it's because it is. Online shopping has plenty of pitfalls, some minor, some possibly major. Here's a summary of the potential downsides to shopping online and what you can and can't do about each of them:

- **The low price isn't really so low with hidden costs.** You can't simply go by the sticker price of products as listed on websites. Be especially careful when ordering from smaller and/or newer websites that may not stand behind what they sell. Shipping costs are often hard to discern and, in the worst cases, not disclosed until after you've invested plenty of your time going through an online checkout process that involves entering lots of personal information. You may also find that the particular colour or style of a product you want is more expensive. Also, be aware that provinces are forcing online retailers to collect provincial sales tax so that cost advantage is disappearing.

- **Online shopping encourages overspending.** Shopping online is easy — too easy. In addition to not even using real cash to buy, you don't even have the sense that you're buying something because when the transaction is complete, all you have is your online receipt. So, for folks with a propensity to overspend, online shopping may be especially problematic.
- **Connection of shopping to social media exposes you to even more advertising and problems.** The online shopping experience is very much intertwined on many sites with social media.
- **On less-than-secure websites, identity theft is a concern.** This is also true on sites set up for the sole purpose of tricking you into revealing your personal and financial details.

* **Bogus and biased online reviews can lead you astray.** Unfortunately, too many online reviews are posted by folks with a vested interest and/or who have never even actually bought and used the product. This is not to say that you can't learn from reading online reviews, but be careful and suspicious, especially with overly flattering reviews.

  TIP: Combat this problem by using Fakespot (`www.fakespot.com`) to determine how authentic or bogus reviews are posted for particular products and services online.

* **If you shop online for the best prices for specific products, you greatly increase the odds of being led to sites that are selling fake merchandise.** Even if what you're buying is the real thing, if you have problems with it, the manufacturer may not stand behind the product in the way that it normally would if you had bought from an authorized retailer.

Get your money back

Take a look around your home for items you never use. Odds are, you have some (maybe even many). Returning such items to where you bought them can be cathartic; it also reduces your home's clutter and puts more money in your pocket.

Also, think about the last several times you bought a product or service and didn't get what was promised. What did you do about it? Most people do nothing and let the derelict company off the hook. Why? Here are some common explanations for this type of behaviour:

- **Low standards:** Consumers have come to expect shoddy service and merchandise because of the common lousy experiences they've had.
- **Conflict avoidance:** Most people shun confrontation. It makes them tense and anxious, and it churns their stomachs.
- **Hassle aversion:** Some companies don't make it easy for complainers to get their money back or obtain satisfaction. To get restitution from some companies, you need the tenacity and determination of a pit bull.

TIP You can increase your odds of getting what you expect for your money by doing business with companies that:

- **Have fair return policies:** Don't purchase any product or service until you understand the company's return policy. Be especially wary of buying from companies that charge hefty "restocking" fees for returned merchandise or simply don't allow returns at all. Reputable companies offer full refunds and don't make you take store credit (although taking credit is fine if you're sure that you'll use it soon and that the company will still be around).

- **Can provide good references:** Suppose that you're going to install a fence on your property, and, as a result, you're going to be speaking with fencing contractors for the first time. You can sift out many inferior firms by asking each contractor that you interview for at least three references from people in your local area who have had a fence installed in the past year or two.
- **Are committed to the type of product or service they provide:** Suppose that your chosen fencing contractor does a great job, and now that you're in the market for new gutters on your home, the contractor says that they do gutters, too. Although the path of least resistance would be to simply hire the same contractor for your gutters, you should inquire about how many gutters the contractor has installed and also interview some other firms that specialize in such work. Because your fencing contractor may have done only a handful of gutter jobs, they may not know as much about that type of work.

TIP

Following these guidelines can greatly diminish your chances of having negative outcomes with products or services you buy. And here's another important tip: Whenever possible and as long as you can pay the balance in full when due, buy with a credit card if your credit's in good standing. Doing so enables you to dispute a charge within 60 days and gives you leverage for getting your money back.

TIP If you find that you're unable to make progress when trying to get compensation for a lousy product or service, here's what you can do:

- **Document.** Taking notes whenever you talk to someone at a company can help you validate your case down the road, if problems develop. Obviously, the bigger the purchase and the more money you have at stake, the more carefully you should document what you've been promised. Try to get into the habit of writing down the name of the person you're speaking with and the time and date of your call. Keep copies of companies' marketing literature, because such documents often make promises or claims that companies fail to live up to in practice.
- **Escalate.** Some frontline employees either aren't capable of resolving disputes or lack the authority to do so. No matter what the cause, speak with a department supervisor and continue escalating from there. If you're still not making progress, lodge a complaint to whatever regulatory agency (if any) oversees such companies.

  Consider posting your beefs on some of the numerous consumer complaint websites and possibly social media outlets, but be careful to stick to the facts and avoid saying something false or incendiary that could lead to your being sued. Tell your friends and colleagues not to do business with the company (and let the company know that you're doing so until your complaint is resolved to your satisfaction).

Also, consider contacting a consumer help group. These groups are typically sponsored by broadcast or print media in metropolitan areas. They can be helpful in resolving disputes or shining a light on disreputable companies or products.

- **Litigate.** If all else fails, consider taking the matter to small-claims court if the company continues to be unresponsive. (Depending on the amount of money at stake, this tactic may be worth your time.) The maximum dollar limit that you may recover in most provinces is $25,000. For larger amounts than those allowed in small-claims court in your province, you can, of course, hire a lawyer and pursue your claim through the traditional legal channels — although you may end up throwing away more of your time and money. Mediation and arbitration are generally better options than following through on a lawsuit.

Cut excess spending

If you want to reduce your overall spending by, say, 10 percent, you can just cut all your current expenditures by 10 percent. Or, you can reach your 10 percent goal by cutting some categories a lot and others not at all. You need to set priorities and make choices about where you want (and don't want) to spend your money.

TIP What you spend your money on is sometimes a matter of habit rather than a matter of what you really want or value. For example, some people shop at whatever stores are close to them. These days, some people order many things online, but that can lead to overspending as well. But eliminating fat doesn't necessarily mean cutting back on your purchases: You can save money by buying in bulk. Some stores specialize in selling larger packages or quantities of a product at a lower price because they save money on the packaging and handling. If you're single, shop with a friend and split the bulk purchases. You can also do some comparison shopping online, but be sure you're surveying reputable websites that stand behind what they sell and that provide high-quality customer service.

Shun consumer credit

As we discuss in Chapter 3, buying items that depreciate — such as cars, clothing, and vacations — on credit is hazardous to your long-term financial health. Buy only what you can afford today. If you'll be forced to carry a debt for months or years on end, you can't afford what you're buying on credit.

Without a doubt, *renting to own* is the most expensive way to buy. Here's how it works: You see a huge ad blaring "$39.99 for a 65-inch smart TV!" Well, the ad has a big hitch: That's $39.99 per week, for many weeks. When all is said and done (and paid), buying a $998 65-inch smart TV through a rent-to-own store costs a typical buyer more than $3,639. Welcome to the world of rent-to-own stores, which offer cash-poor consumers the ability to lease consumer items and, at the end of the lease, an option to buy.

If you think that paying a 20 percent interest rate on a credit card is expensive, consider this: The effective interest rate charged on many rent-to-own purchases exceeds 100 percent; in some cases, it may be 200 percent or more. Renting to own makes buying on a credit card look like a great deal. This information isn't meant to encourage you to buy on credit cards, but to point out what a rip-off renting to own is. Such stores prey on cashless consumers who either can't get credit cards or don't understand how expensive renting to own really is. Forget the instant gratification and save a set amount each week until you can afford what you want.

TIP Consumer credit is expensive, and it reinforces a bad financial habit: spending more than you can afford.

How to Budget to Boost Your Savings

When most people hear the word *budgeting*, they think unpleasant thoughts — like those associated with *dieting* — and rightfully so. But budgeting can help you move from knowing how much you spend on various things to successfully reducing your spending.

The first step in the process of *budgeting*, or planning your future spending, is to analyze where your current spending is going (covered earlier in this chapter). After you do that, calculate how much more you'd like to save each month. Then comes the hard part: deciding where to make cuts in your spending.

Suppose that you're currently not saving any of your monthly income and you want to save 10 percent for retirement. If you can save and invest through a tax-sheltered retirement savings plan, you don't actually need to cut your spending by 10 percent to reach a savings goal of 10 percent (of your gross income). When you contribute money to a tax-deductible Registered Retirement Savings Plan (RRSP), you reduce your federal and provincial taxes. If you're a moderate-income earner paying — say, 35 percent in taxes on your marginal income — you actually need to reduce your spending by only 6.5 percent to save 10 percent. The other 3.5 percent of the savings comes from the lowering of your taxes. (The higher your tax bracket, the less you need to cut your spending to reach a particular savings goal.)

So, to boost your savings rate to 10 percent, go through your current spending category by category until you come up with enough proposed cuts to reduce your spending by 7 percent. Make your cuts in the areas that will be the least painful and where you're getting the least value from your current level of spending.

> Another method of budgeting involves starting completely from scratch rather than examining your current expenses and making cuts from that starting point. Ask yourself how much you'd like to spend on different categories. The advantage of this approach is that it doesn't allow your current spending levels to constrain your thinking. You'll likely be amazed at the discrepancies between what you think you should be spending and what you actually are spending in certain categories.

5

Trimming Your Taxes

The taxes you pay — income tax, sales tax, and federal and provincial taxes — probably add up to more than you realize. Few of us know just how much we pay in taxes each year. We remember being happy when we get an income tax refund, or conversely being not-so-happy if we find out we owed income tax. The purpose of filing a tax return is to settle any differences between the amount of taxes you paid during the year versus the total tax you owe, based on your income and deductions.

The goal of this chapter is to help you legally and permanently reduce your total taxes. Understanding the tax system is the key to reducing your tax burden — if you don't, you'll surely pay more taxes than necessary. Your tax ignorance can also lead to mistakes, which can be costly if the Canada

Revenue Agency (CRA) catches your underpayment errors. And with the proliferation of computerized information and data tracking, discovering mistakes has never been easier.

TIP The amounts noted are all up to date as of the time of writing, and apply for 2022, but be forewarned — they regularly change. Things change, so why should tax forms be any different? The CRA's (Canada Revenue Agency) tax documents, guides, and websites are refreshingly clear, well laid out, and easy-to-follow. If you need more help, information, or instructions, they're a great place to start.

A Look at the Taxes You Pay

Some people feel lucky when they get an income tax refund, but if you do receive a refund, it indicates that you overpaid your income taxes during the year. You should have had this money in your own account all along, earning interest. If you have received large amounts in income tax refunds over the past three years, for example, you should find out why (talk to your employer) and adjust the amount of tax being deducted from your paycheque.

TIP: Instead of focusing on whether you're going to get a refund when you complete your annual tax return, concentrate on the total taxes you pay, which are discussed in this section.

Total taxes

The total taxes payable are determined by completing the arithmetic on the federal T1 General form. When you reach line 43500, "Total Payable," your next step is to subtract all credits — including your provincial tax credits — from your total tax payable, except for tax that you've already had deducted (line 43700) or tax that you've paid in installments (line 47600). You will either have a refund (line 48400) or balance owing (line 48500).

The goal of this chapter is to provide you with tips and strategies to legally reduce your payable taxes, and to keep these tips and strategies in mind to keep taxes to a minimum. One key tip is to read about federal and provincial tax rates and determine where you qualify for credits. Not knowing the tax rules well may lead you to make mistakes, such as underpaying your taxes, or not paying on time, which could incur penalties. Tax software will help reduce errors, as will a call to the CRA if you are uncertain about an aspect of the tax form.

The tax system, like other public policy, is built around incentives to encourage Canadians to think about their financial well-being. For example, saving for retirement is considered desirable because it encourages people to prepare for a time in their lives when they have less income and perhaps have additional healthcare expenses. Therefore, the tax code offers all sorts of tax perks, which are discussed later in this chapter, to encourage people to save in Registered Retirement Savings Plans (RRSPs), registered retirement plans, and other tax-deferred or tax-sheltered plans. This includes Tax-Free Savings Accounts (TFSAs), Registered Education Savings Plans (RESPs), and Registered Disability Savings Plans (RDSPs).

TIP

You should make the choices that work best for your life and situation. However, keep in mind that the *fewer* desirable activities you engage in, the more you'll generally pay in taxes. If you understand the options, you can choose the ones that meet your needs as you approach different stages of your financial life.

Marginal tax rate

When it comes to taxes, not all income is treated equally. This fact is far from self-evident. If you work for an employer and earn a salary, your employer will deduct money from your paycheque to pay federal and provincial taxes owing (whether you're paid by direct deposit or by a physical cheque). The amount of the deduction does not typically vary from payday to payday.

In reality, you pay less tax on your *first* dollars of earnings each year and more tax on your *last* dollars of earnings. For example, if you're single and your taxable income (see the next section) totaled $56,000 in 2022, the first $14,398 is not taxable. It is a tax credit. The federal tax rate is 15 percent on the first $50,197 of taxable income, and if you are a resident of Ontario, the rate is 5.05 percent.

- Federal tax payable: $56,000 - $14,398 x 15% = $6240.30
- Ontario tax payable: $56,000 - $14,398 x 5.05% = $2100.90

TIP: You can obtain the federal, provincial, and territorial tax rates from the CRA website. Your tax rate is a combination of federal and provincial taxes, and each province and territory has different marginal rates, tax brackets, and surtaxes. The result is that taxes are not uniform across the country.

A *marginal tax rate* is the rate of tax you pay on your *last*, or so-called *highest*, dollars of income in the year. In 2022, for example, the federal income tax rate is 15 percent on the first $50,197 of taxable income. If your taxable income is $66,000, the federal tax rate that applies to the difference between $66,000 and $50,197 is 20.5 percent. The Ontario rate that applies is 9.15 percent.

- Federal marginal tax rate: $66,000 - $50,197 x 20.5% = $3239.62
- Ontario marginal tax rate: $66,000 - $50,197 x 9.15% = $1445.98

Although it may seem a little tedious, understanding the impact of marginal tax rates is often very financially rewarding. For example, if your taxable income is close to the higher marginal rate, putting money into your RRSP will result in a deduction and reduce your tax rate to the lower marginal rate.

TIP

For the latest information on tax rates, visit `www.canada.ca/en/revenue-agency/services/tax/individuals/frequently-asked-questions-individuals/canadian-income-tax-rates-individuals-current-previous-years.html#federal`.

Taxable income

Taxable income is the amount of income on which you pay income taxes. (The following sections explain strategies for reducing your taxable income.) Here's why you don't pay taxes on your total income:

- **Not all income is taxable.** For example, any profit you make when you sell the home you live in — your principal residence — generally isn't taxable.

  Withdrawals from TFSAs are also not taxable. Growth in an RRSP is not taxed until such time as withdrawals are made. (As discussed later in this chapter, if you earn interest on money outside such accounts, it's taxed at the same rate as your regular employment income. Other income, such as that from stock dividends and long-term capital gains, is taxed at lower rates.)
- **You get to subtract deductions from your income.** Some deductions are available just for being a living, breathing human being. In 2022, every taxpayer got an automatic exemption — known as the *basic personal amount* — on their first $14,398 of income.
- **Contributions to retirement savings plans are usually deductible.** When you contribute to a qualified retirement plan such as an RRSP, you also effectively get a deduction.

Alternative minimum tax

You may find this hard to believe, but a second tax system exists (as if the first tax system weren't already complicated enough). This second system may increase your taxes above normal levels.

Over the years, wealthy people with complex financial lives, aided by lawyers and accountants, became adept at slashing their tax bill with often-complex deductions, exclusions from taxable income, and loopholes unavailable to most working Canadians. To capture this lost revenue, the government created a second tax system — the *alternative minimum tax* (AMT) — to ensure that those using aggressive tax-minimization strategies pay at least a certain percentage of taxes on their incomes. (The minimum tax does not apply in the year of someone's death.)

Even if you're not claiming a lot of deductions or using tax-sheltered investments such as limited partnerships, you may also get tripped up by AMT. For instance, someone who receives a substantial capital gain — say, a farmer who sells off a large plot of land — may find that the AMT kicks in.

AMT limits the use of certain deductions and requires that 60 percent of the normally untaxed half of any capital gains be added to taxable income. Some so-called *tainted shelter deductions,* including tax shelters and resource write-offs, are also added back. Then, after a $40,000 exemption, federal tax payable is determined. (Most personal tax credits, except for the dividend tax and the investment tax credits, can be used.)

A similar calculation is also used for provincial taxes, with the minimum provincial tax rate ranging anywhere from 35 percent to 55 percent of the federal minimum tax.

When all the number crunching is done, the tax payable is whichever is higher — the AMT or the tax due using the regular system.

TIP: If you do have to pay the higher amount prescribed by the minimum tax calculation, the money may not be gone forever. In the following seven years, you can recover it by the amount your regular tax owing exceeds what you would pay using the minimum tax calculation.

TIP: For more information on AMT, visit `www.canada.ca/en/revenue-agency/services/tax/individuals/topics/about-your-tax-return/tax-return/completing-a-tax-return/deductions-credits-expenses/minimum-tax.html`.

Employment Income Taxes

You're supposed to pay taxes on income you earn from work. Not accounting for all your earnings will reduce your taxable employment income, but you risk being found out and paying penalties and extra interest charges on top of the taxes you owe. And you may even get tossed into jail. Because no one wants you to serve jail time or lose even more money by paying unnecessary penalties and interest, this section focuses on the best *legal* ways to reduce your income taxes on your earnings from work.

Contribute to registered retirement plans

Putting money into an RRSP or employer's pension plan is one of the few painless and government-approved ways to reduce your taxable employment income. Besides reducing your taxes, registered retirement plans help you build up a nest egg so that you can maintain a lifestyle you have planned for when you decide to put your feet up.

You can reduce taxable income by contributing to an RRSP or employer-based retirement plan. If your marginal tax rate is 34 percent and you contribute $1,000 to one of these plans, you reduce your taxes by $340. Do you like the sound of that? How about this: Contribute another $1,000, and your taxes drop another $340 (if you're still in the same marginal tax rate). When that money is inside a retirement plan, it can compound and grow without taxation.

Many people miss this great opportunity to reduce their taxes because they spend all (or too much) of their current employment income and, therefore, have nothing (or little) left to put into a retirement plan. If you're in this predicament, you first need to reduce your spending before you can contribute money to a retirement plan. (Chapter 4 explains how to decrease your spending.)

TIP: If your employer doesn't offer a retirement or pension plan, an RRSP is your best bet. (You may also be able to contribute to an RRSP after contributing the maximum to your employer's pension plan.)

The earlier in life you set up an RRSP, the better, whether you do it through your employer or on your own.

Shift some income

Income shifting, which has nothing to do with money laundering, is a tax-reduction strategy that's an option for those who can control *when* they receive their income.

For example, suppose your employer tells you in late December that you're eligible for a bonus. You're given the option to receive your bonus in December or January. If you're certain that you'll be in a higher tax bracket next year, you should choose to receive your bonus in December.

Or, suppose you run your own business and you think that you'll be in a lower tax bracket next year. Perhaps you plan to take time off to be with a newborn or take an extended trip. You may be able to push a big contract off until January, so the income is earned and, therefore, taxed in the next year.

Get organized

Locating all the scraps of paper you need when completing your tax return can be a hassle. Setting up a filing system can be a big time-saver:

- **Folder or shoebox:** If you have limited patience for setting up neat file folders, and you lead an uncomplicated financial life (that is, you haven't saved receipts throughout the year), you can confine your filing to January and February. During those months, you should receive tax summary statements on wages paid by your employer (T4), taxable dividend income from Canadian corporations (T5), income from profit-sharing plans (T4PS), and interest income (T5 for bank account and regular interest Canada Savings Bond "R" bonds; T5008 for T-bills). If you're older, you may also get a slip for Old Age Security (OAS) income (T4AOAS) and the Canada Pension Plan (CPP) or Quebec Pension Plan (QPP) (T4A[P]). You may also have received a T3 for income from a mutual fund trust.

TIP: You can also set up an account with the CRA and download statements.

Set up a folder that's labelled with something easy to remember (something like "2022 Taxes" would be a brilliant choice) and dump these papers as well as your tax booklet into it. When you're ready to crunch numbers, you should have everything you need to complete the form. You can also scan receipts and statements and keep them in an electronic folder.

- **Accordion-type file:** Organizing the bills you pay into individual folders during the entire year is a more thorough approach. This method is essential if you own your own business and need to tabulate your expenditures for office supplies each year. No one is going to send you a form totalling your office expenditures for the year — you're on your own.
- **Software:** Software programs can help organize your tax information during the year and save you time and accounting fees come tax-prep time.

How to Increase Your Deductions

Deductions are amounts you subtract from your adjusted gross income before calculating the tax you owe. To determine just what a deduction is worth, multiply it by your marginal tax rate. The following sections detail some of the more common deductions you may be able to take advantage of.

Childcare expenses

Many of the costs of having others take care of your children can be deducted from your income. Babysitters, day nurseries, day care, and day camps, all qualify, as do boarding school fees (outside of education costs) and the cost of overnight camps, up to set maximums. However, the expenses must be incurred to enable you either to work or to take an occupational training course.

You can deduct up to $8,000 of expenses for each child who is under age 7 at the end of the year, and up to $5,000 for each child ages 7 to 16. In most cases, if you are married, only the lower-earning spouse can claim these expenses. Further, the total deduction can't be greater than two-thirds of the salary or net business income (technically, earned income) of the lower-earning spouse or the single parent. (The limits are higher for children with disabilities.)

For Quebec residents, childcare expenses give you a refundable credit, not a deduction, and different limits apply.

Alimony and maintenance payments

Alimony or maintenance payments you make to a former spouse can be deducted if they're made following a decree, order, judgement, or written agreement. To be deductible, they must be an allowance that is paid out in regular, predetermined payments. You can't deduct any transfers of property or one-time payments you make as part of a settlement.

Annual union and professional fees

Regular annual dues (often taken off automatically from your paycheque) are deductible, but you can't claim initiation fees, licences, or special assessments. Fees paid to professional organizations are deductible, but only if they must be paid to maintain a professional standing recognizable by law, such as a registered nurse. This applies even if maintaining that status isn't required by your current job. If you're self-employed, you can generally deduct dues you pay to voluntarily belong to work-related organizations.

Business losses

You can use losses from an unincorporated business or professional practice to reduce your employment or professional income. Say that you have a salaried job, and you possess a degree in music. You decide to teach piano, which requires buying or leasing a piano, music books, and so on. If your music business expenses are greater than the income teaching earns, you can subtract your loss from your salaried income.

Interest on investment loans

If you borrow money to buy investments or to earn income from a business, the interest can be deducted. (This rule doesn't apply to money borrowed to make an RRSP contribution.) You'll need to keep a record of any money you borrow that you use to make investments and track the amount of interest you pay.

Moving expenses

Not only is moving a major hassle, but it can be costly, so eligible moving expenses can be a valuable deduction. The costs to move when you are required to relocate for business can be claimed as a deduction. Check for minimum requirements on the distance of the move. Moving to Canada from another country — or moving from Canada *to* another country — doesn't qualify.

Eligible expenses include the travelling costs to move you and your family (including food and lodging along the way) and your household belongings, as well as any related storage costs. In addition, you can deduct the cost of selling your old home, including the real estate commissions, and the legal bills on purchasing your new home.

TIP

Expenses can be deducted only against income that is earned in the new location. If you're unable to deduct all the expenses in the year of the move, the remainder can be deducted in future years. So, don't forget to carry that deduction forward.

It's often overlooked, but students are also eligible to claim this deduction if they move so they can attend university or another postsecondary institution full-time. The expenses must be deducted against taxable scholarships, bursaries, research grants, or fellowships. Students can also claim moving expenses if the move is in order to take a job — including a summer job — or to start a business. Expenses can be claimed each time the student returns after the summer break, or from a work semester.

New working from home deduction

The federal government introduced a temporary deduction for employees who worked from home due to the COVID-19 pandemic. To qualify, you must have worked from home at least 50 percent of the time for a minimum of four weeks in a row. You can claim $2 per day you worked from home, up to a maximum of $400 for 2020, and $500 for both 2021 and 2022. No documents are required from either you or your employers for this flat-rate method.

If your expenses are higher, you should consider using the alternate, detailed method. This allows you to claim the actual amounts you paid. However, you must have receipts or other documents to support those payments, as well as a signed declaration from your employer that you worked from home due to COVID-19.

Tax Credits

Tax credits are different from deductions in one fundamental and important way. Deductions are subtracted from your income *before* your tax bill is calculated. This means a deduction saves you the amount of the deduction multiplied by your marginal tax rate. Suppose you have a deduction of $200. If your marginal tax rate is 30 percent, you'll cut $60 from your tax bill ($200 x 0.30).

In contrast, credits only come into play *after* your taxable income has been arrived at, and your tax bill calculated. Credits are then applied against your tax bill, as though you've already paid that amount in taxes. As a result, your taxes are reduced by the full amount of the credit. A $500 credit is worth the same amount to everybody regardless of their level of income or tax bracket — it reduces the tax owed by $500.

TIP

Most credits are *non-refundable.* At best, they can reduce your tax bill to zero, but they won't put more money in your pocket. If you have $1,200 in credits left over after bringing your federal tax payable to zero, that's as good as it gets. The government won't send you a cheque for $1,200.

How the federal and provincial tax systems work together

All the provinces (except Quebec) calculate your provincial tax bill by applying their marginal rates directly to your taxable income. This is known as the *tax on net income* (TONI) method. With this method, the federal and provincial governments calculate your taxes by multiplying your income by their respective tax rate. You then separately deduct your federal and provincial tax credits from the corresponding gross tax payable to arrive at your basic federal and basic provincial tax.

Previously, provincial taxes were calculated as a percentage of your basic federal tax bill; this was known as the *tax-on-tax method.* Credits were generally deducted from your federal tax bill before your provincial taxes and surtaxes were calculated. With the old tax-on-tax system, tax credits were worth from 50 percent to 70 percent more than the straight federal credit. By cutting your federal taxes, you also reduced your provincial taxes and surtaxes.

When the provinces moved to the TONI method, they were required to maintain the basic credits that are offered at the federal level. The value of a federal credit will be about 40 percent to 70 percent more when the provincial tax credit is added.

How to maximize your tax credits

The following sections outline some common credits that may be available to you and your family and include some tips on how to maximize them. Check your tax guide for the specific amounts for the year you're filing.

Basic personal tax credit

Everyone gets a basic federal credit, which for individuals who earn less than $155,625 in 2022 was $14,398.

Spousal credit

You can claim a federal spousal credit of $14,398, and the amount claimed can vary depending on income.

If you supported your spouse at any point in the year, and they earn less than the basic personal amount, you can claim the non-refundable spousal tax credit. (If your spouse or common-law partner was dependent on you because of a mental or physical impairment, you can use the credit if their income was lower than your basic personal amount plus $2,350.)

TIP: You can claim this amount for the entire year, even if you met the eligibility requirements for only part of the year.

If the lower-earning partner makes more than the cut-off amount, they may still be able to get under the income threshold by making an RRSP contribution.

Amount for an eligible dependant

You can claim this credit if you are single, separated, divorced, or widowed, you support an eligible dependant who lives with you, and their net income was less than your basic personal amount. (This used to be known as the *equivalent-to-spouse credit.*) If they were dependent due to a physical or mental impairment, that cut-off amount is bumped up by $2,295.

A parent or grandparent qualifies as an eligible dependant. So does a child, grandchild, brother, or sister (by blood, marriage, common-law partnership, or adoption) if they were under 18 years old. (The age limit doesn't apply if the person is dependent on you because of a mental or physical disability.)

Climate action incentive

If you live in Saskatchewan, Manitoba, Ontario, or Alberta, you can claim the Climate Action Incentive (CAI). The CAI was brought in to offset the fuel charge that these four provinces add directly to the cost of your gas (whether it's heating bills or at the gas station). In most cases, the average household will benefit.

You're allowed one credit per household and the amount you receive is based on the size of your family. If you live in British Columbia, you can generally claim the BC Climate Action Tax Credit (issued with your GST/HST Tax Credit), which helps low-income individuals and families offset the carbon taxes they pay.

Credits for charitable donations

You can earn credits from most contributions made to charities if you get an official tax receipt. In addition to cash contributions, you can often claim donations of items of value, such as a used computer. The amount of the receipt must reflect the item's fair market value. However, you can't get a receipt for your time or the expenses you ring up while doing charitable work.

The charitable tax credit is non-refundable, and it is available federally and from your province. The first $200 you donate earns you a 15 percent federal tax credit. After your savings on provincial taxes are accounted for, this works out to be worth about 25 percent. For donations beyond the $200 level, though, your donations give you a 29 percent federal tax credit, worth about 46 percent after the savings on provincial taxes are counted. (This makes your donations above $200 worth almost as much as a deduction if you're in the top tax bracket.)

Finally, if you are in the top tax bracket, your donation gives you a 33 percent federal tax credit. When the provincial credit is factored in, this translates to a 50 percent value. (This rate only applies to any donations above $200 up to the amount your income exceeds a set ceiling.)

Even if the credit won't save you in taxes, it's always wise to make sure any charity you're thinking of donating to is genuine. An official-looking fraudulent charities take your money and offer you a fake tax receipt. There are always traditional and new donation scams being promoted by unscrupulous fraudsters. Find out if any charity you want to help out is legitimate by searching the CRA's list of registered charities at `https://apps.cra-arc.gc.ca/ebci/hacc/srch/pub/dsplyBscSrch?request_locale=en`.

Avoid any group that issues you a tax receipt for more than your donation. This is illegal and will likely get you into trouble with the tax authorities. And your money won't go to the cause you want to support.

TIP

If you donate only small amounts to charities each year, try to pool several years' contributions to put you over the $200 donation level. You can also combine your spouse's and your own contributions on one return. This prevents both of you from having to get the lower credit on the first $200. Note that you don't have to claim a charitable deduction in the year that it's made. Unclaimed contributions can be carried forward and claimed on your return in any of the five years after the year in which you make the charitable contribution. Also, if you're already over $200 in donations and plan to make further donations in the new year, instead of waiting, make them by the end of

December of the current year if possible. This will allow you to receive the tax savings a year earlier.

Medical expenses credit

A surprisingly wide range of medical costs and health-related expenditures are eligible for a non-refundable credit. You can find the full list on the CRA website. Here are some of the key items to be aware of:

- Air conditioners for someone with severe chronic ailment, disease, or disorder (amount capped, prescription required).
- Ambulance service to/from public or licensed private hospitals.
- Artificial limbs or eyes.
- Baby breathing monitors. A written certificate from medical practitioner must certify an infant at risk of sudden infant death syndrome (prescription required).
- Bathroom aids to assist in use of the bathtub, shower, or toilet (prescription required).
- Breast prostheses because of mastectomy (prescription required).
- Certificate fees. The fees for completion of Disability Tax Credit Certificate (Form T2201) and other certificates.

- Dental services, dentures, and dental implants (purely cosmetic procedures not eligible).
- Diapers and disposable briefs for incontinence from illness, injury, or affliction.
- Doctor/physician expenses (see the CRA website for details, varies by province).
- Fertility-related procedures. Includes medical practitioner and public and licensed private hospital fees to conceive a child (payments to surrogate mothers not generally eligible).
- Gluten-free food products. People with celiac disease can claim incremental costs of gluten-free food products. (Generally limited to food produced and marketed for gluten-free diets, such as gluten-free bread.)
- Insulin, needles, syringes, and infusion pumps for diabetics.
- Laboratory fees, procedures, and services, including necessary interpretations (prescription required).
- Medical aids, including wheelchairs, hearing aids and batteries, crutches, braces, and guide dogs (including their care).
- Medical cannabis. Purchaser must have a document from a healthcare practitioner for medical use of cannabis and buy from licensed seller where they're a

registered client. (Holder of certificate allowing production of cannabis for personal medical use cannot deduct costs of oil, fertilizer, pots, and lights.)

- Moving expenses. Reasonable and unclaimed expenses to move someone with severe and prolonged mobility impairment, or who lacks normal physical development, to more accessible housing, or housing that makes them more mobile or functional. Maximum $2,000. (In Ontario, this is $3,009.)
- Orthodontic work, including braces, performed by medical practitioner or dentist. Purely cosmetic procedures ineligible.
- Orthopaedic shoes, boots, and inserts (prescription required).
- Pre- and post-natal treatments and in vitro fertility treatments.
- Prescription drugs and medications.
- Prescription eyeglasses, contact lenses, swimming goggles, and print-reading aids (devices/software) (prescription required).
- Private health services plan premiums.
- Travel expenses to receive medical care outside local community.

You can claim eligible medical expenses paid in any 12-month period ending in 2021 and not claimed for 2020.

Generally, you can claim all amounts paid that are more than a certain threshold, even if they were not paid in Canada. Medical expenses for other dependants must be claimed on line 33199 of your return.

After totalling your expenses, you can claim only the amount that exceeds 3 percent of your net income or $2,421, whichever is lower.

To maximize the benefit of this credit, one spouse can and should claim the entire family's medical expenses. The spouse with the lowest income generally should make the claim, to get over the 3-percent floor as quickly as possible. Plus, in any tax year, you can claim your expenses for any 12 months ending in that particular year. If you have a lot of bills in the fall and spring, for example, it may pay to make your claim run from August 1 to July 31.

TIP

You can include a broad range of medical costs in calculating this credit. Add any payments to doctors, nurses, dentists, and public or licenced private hospitals for medical or dental care. In addition, you can include payments for any prescription drugs and medications, eyeglasses, and therapy for speech or hearing problems. You can also include any premiums for private health insurance plans. (That includes the cost of travel insurance for your vacations out of the country.) You can't claim any expenses that you're reimbursed for from, say, a company dental plan, but any deductibles you pay do qualify.

TIP

Low-income earners who have high medical bills may also be able to take advantage of the *medical expense supplement*. For 2021, the maximum supplement is the lesser of $1,285 or 25 percent of medical expenses (line 33200 of the federal tax return) and disability support expenses (line 21500).

If you live in Quebec, the 3-percent mark your medical expenses must exceed in order to be claimable is based not on your individual income, but on your family income. Quebec defines your family income as the combined net income of you and your spouse. And, unlike the federal 3 percent, there is no limit on the 3-percent threshold in Quebec.

Pension income credit

You can claim a federal credit of 15 percent for a small amount of certain types of pension income, called *qualifying pension income*. This generally means payments that are received from a private pension. If you're 65 or older, or you're receiving benefits due to your spouse's death, other income also qualifies. This includes payments from a Registered Retirement Income Fund (RRIF), the income portion of a regular annuity, and payments from annuities from an RRSP or deferred profit-sharing plan also qualify. CPP, OAS, or Guaranteed Income Supplement (GIS) payments do not qualify. Currently, the federal tax credit is worth 15 percent on the first $2,000 of qualifying pension income. If you're unable to use the credit, it may be transferred to your spouse. To make use of this credit, try to have at least $2,000 of qualifying pension income each year, if possible, as well as an additional $2,000 for your spouse.

Age 65 or older

If you're 65 or older by the end of the year, you can claim a federal tax credit — the *age credit*. For 2021, the maximum was $7,713, and to qualify, your net income must not exceed $89,422. The amount a senior can claim is assessed against their income.

Disability credit

You're eligible for a non-refundable federal credit if you have a severe and prolonged mental or physical impairment. The federal disability tax credit is 15 percent of the base amount. The base amount maximum for 2021 is $8,662, and 15 percent of that amount is $1,299.30. A supplemental amount for children with disabilities is calculated according to the Canada Revenue Agency Indexation Chart. Depending on the type of disability, it must be certified by the relevant professional (medical doctor, optometrist, audiologist, occupational therapist, or psychologist).

If a dependent relative doesn't earn enough income to use all their disability credit, a supporting relative can use any unused amount. The eligible dependant can be a spouse, child, grandchild, parent, grandparent, sibling, aunt, uncle, niece, or nephew. In addition, lower-income families caring for a child eligible for the disability tax credit may also qualify for Child Disability Benefit payments.

Families that care for children with severe disabilities can also receive a supplementary credit, and if a parent supports a disabled child who is over 18 years old, the parent is allowed an additional federal credit. The amount that can be claimed may be reduced by other tax credits being claimed or by income earned that exceeds the minimum threshold.

Canada caregiver credit

In 2017, the Canada caregiver credit replaced three longstanding credits: the infirm dependant credit, the caregiver credit (for in-home care of a relative), and the family caregiver credit.

You can claim the caregiver credit if, at any time during the year, your spouse or common-law partner, a minor child, another eligible relative, or a dependant of your partner is dependent on you because of a physical or mental infirmity.

Unlike the old credit rules, it's not required that your dependant lives with you, but the person has to be dependent on you for "support," which includes basic necessities such as food, shelter, and clothing.

Obtain a Disability Tax Certificate from a doctor or nurse practitioner.

Previously, you were generally eligible for the credit for supporting a parent who lived with you and was at least 65, but who did not have a medical condition. However, there is no longer a credit for non-infirm parents over 65 who live with you.

The caregiver credit is non-refundable, meaning it can reduce your taxes all the way to zero, but it won't get you a refund. (You might end up with a refund, but that's only because you've paid too much tax during the year.)

The maximum credit amount is currently $7,348. However, the credit is reduced dollar for dollar for the parent's income and becomes zero if the dependant's income reaches $24,604.

There is a second lower maximum credit (previously, the family caregiver amount) of $2,295 that may apply. This lower level applies if, for the disabled dependant, you've also claimed the credit for

- A spouse or common-law partner
- An eligible dependant
- A disabled child under age 18

If claiming this second, lower maximum leaves you paying more taxes than you would have if the first, higher amount had been claimed, you get a top-up amount that offsets any difference.

British Columbia, Ontario, and Yukon have corresponding credits. The other provinces, however, have stuck with the older caregiver amount, which provides a credit if your parent lives with you and is 65 or older, or if you're caring for an infirm adult relative.

The exchange of consumer debt for mortgage debt

If you've run up high-interest consumer debt, and you own a home or other real estate and you haven't borrowed the maximum, you may be able to take on some low-cost debt to pay off some high-cost debt. You can save on interest charges by refinancing your mortgage or taking out a home-equity loan at a lower rate and putting the cash toward paying off your credit card, auto loan, or other costly credit lines.

You must exercise discipline and not allow borrowing against the equity in your home to become a habit. Never think of equity in your home as a way to run up credit cards or make unnecessary purchases.

Having equity in your home may create the illusion that excess spending isn't really taking on debt. But debt is debt, and all borrowed money ultimately has to be repaid (unless you file for bankruptcy). In the long run, you wind up with greater mortgage debt, and paying it off takes a bigger bite out of your monthly income. Refinancing and establishing home equity lines of credit costs you more in terms of loan application fees and other charges (points, appraisals, credit reports, and so on).

At a minimum, refinancing your mortgage handicaps your ability to work toward other financial goals. In the worst case, easy access to borrowing encourages bad spending habits that can ultimately lead to bankruptcy or foreclosure on your home if you fail to meet your mortgage payments.

The deduction of self-employment expenses

When you're self-employed, you can deduct home office expenses related to running that business from your income before calculating the tax you owe. For example, if you buy a computer or office furniture, you can deduct those expenses. (Sometimes they need to be gradually deducted, or *depreciated,* over time.) Salaries for your employees, payments to casual or contract help, office supplies, rent or mortgage interest for your office space, and phone/communications expenses are also generally deductible.

Many self-employed folks are not aware of all of the deductions they're eligible for and should do the necessary research to become better informed. Others are worried that by claiming legitimate but perhaps large deductions will increase the risk of an audit by the CRA. You must learn more about tax deductions and take full advantage of them. Eligible deductions save you money.

The following are common mistakes made by self-employed people:

- **Being an island unto yourself:** When you're self-employed, not seeking professional tax advice may cost you money. Make the tax laws work for you, rather than against you, by hiring an accountant. (See "Professional help" later in this chapter for information on hiring tax advisors.)
- **Making administrative tax screwups:** As a self-employed individual, you're responsible for the timely filing of all taxes owed on your income and remitting the taxes of any employees. You must calculate and remit tax payments on a quarterly basis, which requires withholding taxes from each employee's paycheque and making timely payments to the CRA. In addition to federal and provincial income taxes, you also need to withhold and send in CPP or QPP contributions and Employment Insurance (EI) premiums.
- **Failing to document expenses:** When you pay with cash, producing the paper trail for cash purchases for the business can be hard (and for the CRA if you're ever audited). At the end of the year, how are you going to remember how much you spent for parking or client meals if you fail to keep a record? How will you survive a CRA audit without proper documentation?

Debit cards are widely accepted and provide a convenient paper trail. (Be careful about getting a debit card in your business's name, though, because some banks don't offer protection against fraudulent use of business debit cards.) Otherwise, you need a record of your daily petty cash purchases. Most pocket calendars or daily organizers include ledgers that allow you to track these small purchases. (Some apps can help with this as well.)

If you aren't that organized, at least get receipts for cash transactions and write on each receipt what the purchase was for. Then stash the receipts in a file folder in your office. Or, better yet, put receipts in envelopes labelled with the month and year. You can also keep a record of your receipts by taking a picture with your smartphone; just be sure to back up your photos regularly.

- **Failing to fund a retirement plan:** You should be saving money toward retirement anyway, and you can't beat the tax break. People who are self-employed are allowed to contribute up to 18 percent of their net income to an RRSP. (This amount is capped each year at a set dollar amount, which currently is $27,830.) If they also belong to a registered pension plan, the maximum amount they're allowed to contribute is decreased by a pension adjustment.

- **Failing to use numbers to help manage business:** If you're a small business owner who doesn't track income, expenses, staff performance, and customer data on a regular basis, your tax return may be the one and only time during the year when you take a financial snapshot of your business. After you go through all the time, trouble, and expense to file your tax return, make sure you reap the rewards of all your work; use those numbers to help analyze and manage your business.

  TIP: Some bookkeepers and tax preparers can provide you with management information reports on your business from the tax data they compile for you. Just ask. (See "Software and websites" later in this chapter for recommendations.)

- **Failing to pay family help:** If your children, spouse, or other relatives help with some aspect of your business, consider paying them for the work. Besides showing them that you value their work, this practice may reduce your family's tax liability. For example, children are usually in a lower tax bracket. By shifting some of your income to family members, you not only cut your tax bill, but also can make them eligible for attractive savings options like an RRSP.

Help from Tax Resources

There are all sorts of ways to prepare your tax return. Which approach makes sense for you depends on the complexity of your situation and your knowledge of taxes.

Regardless of the approach you use, you should be taking financial steps during the year to reduce your taxes. By the time you file your return in the following year, it's often too late for you to take advantage of many tax reduction strategies.

CRA assistance

If you have a straightforward tax return, preparing it and filing it on your own is cost efficient. It will take time to organize the receipts and information slips, patience to complete a rough draft of the return and then complete a final return, and a bit more time to scan or photocopy the final return for your records (or print the fillable PDF).

TIP

While you will follow the CRA's guidelines in completing the return, the CRA has been known to give *incorrect* information from time to time. When you call the CRA with a question, be sure to take notes about your conversation to protect yourself in the event of an audit. Date your notes and include the name and identification number of the tax employee you talked to, the questions you asked, and the employee's responses. File your notes in a folder with a copy of your completed return. To reach the CRA with your questions, call 800-959-8281.

TIP

In addition to the standard instructions that come with your tax return, the CRA offers a number of free and helpful tax guides that you can access online or have delivered to you by calling the CRA. These guides serve as useful references and provide more detail and insight than the basic CRA publications. For the self-employed, many booklets are available depending on your occupation, including *Business and Professional Income, Farming Income, Fishing Income,* and *Rental Income.* Other guides deal with specific circumstances. To inquire about and request these documents, call 800-959-2221 or go to `www.canada.ca/en/revenue-agency.html`.

The CRA has also launched a new online course that explains the tax system and walks you through how to complete a basic return. Like many other CRA and Government of Canada online resources, it is well-written, clear, and easy to follow. You can find it at `www.canada.ca/en/revenue-agency/services/tax/individuals/educational-programs.html`.

Preparation and advice guides

Books about tax preparation and tax planning that highlight common problem areas and are written in clear, simple English are invaluable. They supplement the official instructions not only by helping you complete your return correctly but also by showing you how to save as much money as possible.

Check out *Tax Planning for You and Your Family* prepared by KPMG and published by Thomson Carswell for easy-to-understand, digestible explanations and advice. Another accounting firm, Raymond Chabot Grant Thornton, also has a helpful *Tax Planning Guide,* which you can download at `http://en.planiguide.ca`.

Software and websites

Good tax preparation software can be very helpful. StudioTax, available for free at `www.studiotax.com`, regardless of your income level, is a great, easy-to-use program. TurboTax and H&R Block Tax Software are also programs that are rated as very good. If you go the software route, have a good tax advice book by your side.

Finally, the CRA's website (`www.canada.ca/en/revenue-agency.html`) is among the better tax websites, believe it or not.

Professional help

Competent tax preparers and advisors can save you money — sometimes more than enough to pay their fees — by identifying tax-reduction strategies you may overlook. They can also help reduce the likelihood of an audit, which can be triggered by blunders. Mediocre and lousy tax preparers, on the other hand, may make mistakes and be unaware of sound ways to reduce your tax bill.

Tax practitioners come with varying backgrounds, training, and credentials. The three main types of tax practitioners are preparers, Chartered Professional Accountants (CPAs), and tax lawyers. The more training and specialization a tax practitioner has (and the more affluent their clients), the higher their hourly fee usually is. Fees and competence vary greatly.

TIP: If you hire a tax advisor and you're not sure of the quality of the work performed or the soundness of the advice, consider getting a second opinion. Get a referral from a trusted friend, family member, or entrepreneur (if you are self-employed).

Preparers

Preparers generally have the least amount of training of all the tax practitioners, and a large proportion of them work part-time. As with financial planners, no national regulations apply to preparers, and no licensing is required.

Preparers are appealing because they're relatively inexpensive — they can do most basic returns for around $100 or so. The drawback of using a preparer is that you may hire someone who lacks the knowledge or experience to maximize deductions.

> Preparers make the most sense for folks who do not have a lot of investments, real estate, and so on, who are budget-minded, and who dislike doing their own taxes. If you're not good about hanging on to receipts or you don't want to keep your own files with background details about your taxes, you should shop around for a tax preparer who's committed to the business. You may need all that stuff someday for an audit, and many tax preparers keep and organize their clients' documentation rather than return everything each year. Also, going with a firm that's open year-round may be a safer option (some small shops are open only during tax season) in case tax questions or problems arise.

Chartered Professional Accountants

If you have a more complex return, a CPA is often a better choice. Many CPAs have large personal income tax practices and may also have expertise in preparing returns for small businesses. A professional who is familiar with your business category may be able to give you more complete advice on opportunities for saving and how to organize your business to minimize your tax bill. What's more, they will likely be able to do your return more quickly, meaning a lower bill.

CPAs don't close when the tax season ends. That means you can go to them for advice and help on your schedule, and you'll be able to get help if you have problems after filing your return.

Fees for CPAs vary tremendously. Many charge around $125 to $200 per hour, but CPAs at large companies and in areas with a high cost of living tend to charge somewhat more (sometimes significantly more). Fees for a straightforward return should be less than $500, while a more complex return (for example, a part-time business or investment income) typically costs upwards of a thousand dollars or more.

TIP

If you're self-employed and/or you file lots of other schedules, you may want to hire a CPA. But you don't need to do so every year. If your situation grows complex one year and then stabilizes, consider getting help for the perplexing year and then using preparation guides, software, or a lower-cost preparer in the future.

Tax lawyers

Tax lawyers deal with complicated tax problems and issues that usually have some legal aspect that requires their analysis and opinion. Unless you're a super-high-income earner with a complex financial life, hiring a tax lawyer to prepare your annual return is prohibitively expensive. In fact, many tax lawyers don't prepare returns, but they may offer tax preparation as an ancillary service through others in their office.

You may sometimes need to hire a tax lawyer to avoid running into issues with the CRA, but prepare ahead of time to keep the cost of their advice as low as possible (tax lawyers tend to have the highest hourly billing rates of $250 per hour and up).

6

Important Investment Concepts

Making wise investments doesn't have to be complicated. However, many investors get bogged down in the morass of the thousands of investment choices out there and the often conflicting perspectives on how to invest. This chapter helps you grasp the important bigger-picture issues that can help you ensure that your investment plan meshes with your needs and the realities of the investment marketplace.

The Establishment of Your Goals

Before you select a specific investment, first determine your investment needs and goals. Why are you saving money? What are you going to use it for? You don't need to earmark every dollar, but you should set some major objectives. Establishing objectives is important because the expected use of the money helps you determine how long to invest it. And that, in turn, helps you determine which investments to choose.

The risk level of your investments should factor in your time frame and your comfort level. Investing in high-risk vehicles doesn't make sense if you'll need to spend the funds within the next few years or if you'll have to spend all your profits on stress-induced medical bills.

For example, suppose you've been accumulating money for a down payment on a home you want to buy in a few years. You can't afford much risk with that money because you're going to need it sooner rather than later. Putting that money in the stock market, then, is foolish. As discussed later in this chapter, the stock market can drop a lot in a year or over several years, so stocks are probably too risky a place to invest money you plan to use soon.

Perhaps you're saving toward a longer-term goal, such as retirement, that's 20 or 30 years away. In this case, you're in a position to make riskier investments, because your holdings have more time to bounce back from temporary losses or setbacks. You may want to consider investing in growth investments, such as stocks, within a retirement plan that you leave alone for 20 years or longer. You can tolerate year-to-year volatility in the market — you have time on your side.

If you haven't yet done so, take a tour through Chapter 2, which helps you contemplate and set your financial goals.

The Primary Investments

For a moment, forget all the buzzwords, jargon, and product names you've heard tossed around in the investment world — in many cases, they obscure, sometimes intentionally, what an investment really is and hide the hefty fees and commissions.

Imagine a world with only two investment flavours — think of chocolate and vanilla ice cream. The investment world is really just as simple. You have only two major investment choices: You can be a lender or an owner.

Lending investments

You're a lender when you invest your money in a guaranteed investment certificate (GIC), a Treasury bill, a term deposit, or a bond issued by a company like Bombardier. In each case, you lend your money to an organization — a bank, the federal government, or a company. You're paid an agreed-upon rate of interest for lending your money. The organization also promises to have your original investment (the *principal*) returned to you on a specific date.

Getting paid all the interest in addition to your original investment (as promised) is the best that can happen with a lending investment. Given that the investment landscape is littered with carcasses of failed investments, this is not a result to take for granted.

The worst that can happen with a lending investment is that you don't get everything you were promised. Promises can be broken under extenuating circumstances. When a company goes bankrupt, for example, you can lose all or part of your original investment.

Another risk associated with lending investments is that even if you get what you were promised, the ravages of inflation may reduce the purchasing power of your money. Also, the value of a bond may drop below what you paid for it if interest rates rise or the quality or risk of the issuing company declines.

Table 6-1 shows the reduction in the purchasing power of your money at varying rates of inflation after just ten years.

Inflation Rate	Reduction in Purchasing Power after Ten Years
2%	–18%
4%	–32%
6%	–44%
8%	–54%
10%	–61%

Table 6-1: *Reduction in Purchasing Power Due to Inflation*

TIP

Some investors make the common mistake of thinking that they're diversifying their long-term investment money by buying several bonds, some GICs, and an annuity. The problem, however, is that all these investments pay a relatively low fixed rate of return that's exposed to the vagaries of inflation.

A final drawback to lending investments is that you don't share in the success of the organization to which you lend your money. If the company doubles or triples in size and profits, your principal and interest rate don't double or triple in size along with it; they stay the same. Of course, such success does ensure that you'll get your promised interest and principal.

Ownership investments

You're an *owner* when you invest your money in an asset, such as a company or real estate, that can generate earnings or profits. Suppose that you own 100 shares of Canadian National Railway (CNR) stock. With hundreds of millions of shares of stock outstanding, CNR is a mighty big company — your 100 shares represent a tiny piece of it. What do you get for your small slice of CNR? As a stockholder, although you don't get free train tickets, you do share in the profits of the company in the form of annual dividends and an increase (you hope) in the stock price if the company grows and becomes more profitable. Of course, you receive these benefits if things are going well. If CNR's business declines, your stock may be worth less (or even worthless).

Real estate is another favourite, financially rewarding and time-honoured ownership investment. Real estate can produce profits when it's rented out for more than the expense of owning the property or sold at a price higher than what you paid for it. Numerous successful real estate investors have earned excellent long-term profits.

The value of real estate depends not only on the particulars of the individual property but also on the health and performance of the local economy. When companies in the community are growing and more jobs are being produced at higher wages, real estate often does well. When local employers are laying people off and excess housing is sitting vacant because of previous overbuilding, rent and property values fall, as they did in the late 2000s.

Finally, many Canadians have also built substantial wealth through small business. According to *Forbes* magazine, more of the world's wealthiest individuals have built their wealth through their stakes in small businesses (that became bigger) than through any other vehicle. Small business is the engine that drives much of the country's economic growth. You can participate in small business in a variety of ways: You can start your own business, buy and operate an existing business, or simply invest in promising small businesses.

Investment Returns

The previous section describes the difference between ownership and lending investments. "That's all well and good," you say, "but how do I choose which type of investments to put my money into? How much can I make, and what are the risks?"

Good questions. You can start with the returns you *might* make. This requires looking at history, and history is a record of the past. Using history to predict the future — especially the near future — is dangerous. History may repeat itself, but not always in exactly the same fashion, and not necessarily when you expect it to.

During the past century, ownership investments such as stocks and investment real estate returned around 9 percent per year, handily beating lending investments such as bonds (around 5 percent) and savings accounts (roughly 2 percent to 3 percent) in the investment performance race. Inflation has averaged about 3 percent per year.

If you already know that the stock market can be risky, you may be wondering why investing in stocks is worth the anxiety and potential losses. Why bother for a few extra percent per year? Well, over many years, a few extra percent per year can magnify the growth of your money (see Table 6-2). The more years you have to invest, the greater the difference a few percent make in your returns.

At This Rate of Return on $10,000 Invested	You'll Have This Much in 25 Years	You'll Have This Much in 40 Years
3% (savings account)	$20,938	$32,620
5% (bond)	$33,864	$70,400
9% (stocks and investment real estate)	$86,231	$314,094

Table 6-2: *The Difference a Few Percent Makes*

TIP

Investing is not a spectator sport. You can't earn good returns on stocks and real estate if you keep your money in cash on the sidelines. If you invest in growth investments such as stocks and real estate, don't chase one new investment after another trying to beat the market average returns. The biggest value comes from being in the market, not from beating it.

Investment Risks

Many investors have a simplistic understanding of what risk means and how to apply it to their investment decisions. For example, when compared to the yo-yo motions of the stock market, a bank savings account may seem like a less risky place to put your money. Over the long term, however, the stock market usually beats the rate of inflation, while the interest rate on a savings account does not, especially when factoring in taxes. Thus, if you're saving your money for a long-term goal like retirement, a savings account can be a "riskier" place to put your money if you're concerned about the future purchasing power of your investments.

TIP Before you invest, ask yourself these questions:

- **What am I saving and investing this money for?** In other words, what's my goal?
- **What is my timeline for this investment?** When will I use this money?
- **What is the historical volatility of the investment I'm considering?** Does that suit my comfort level and timeline for this investment?

After you answer these questions, you'll have a better understanding of risk and you'll be able to match your savings goals to their most appropriate investment vehicles. Chapter 2 helps you consider your savings goals and timeline. The following sections address investment risk and returns.

The risks of stocks and bonds

Given the relatively higher historic returns mentioned for ownership investments earlier in this chapter, some people think they should put all their money in stocks and real estate. So, what's the catch?

The risk with ownership investments is the short-term fluctuations in their value. During the last century, stocks declined, on average, by more than 10 percent once every five years. Drops in stock prices of more than 20 percent occurred, on average, once every ten years. Real estate prices suffer similar periodic setbacks.

TIP

Therefore, in order to earn those generous long-term returns from ownership investments like stocks and real estate, you must be willing to tolerate volatility. You absolutely should *not* put all your money in the stock or real estate market. Investing your emergency money or money you expect to use within the next five years in such volatile investments is not a good idea.

The shorter the time period that you have for holding your money in an investment, the less likely growth-oriented investments like stocks are to beat out lending-type investments like bonds. Table 6-3 illustrates the historical relationship between stock and bond returns based on number of years held.

Number of Years the Investment Is Held	Likelihood of Stocks Beating Bonds
1	60%
5	70%
10	80%
20	91%
30	99%

Table 6-3: *Stocks versus Bonds*

TIP

Some types of bonds have higher yields than others, but the risk–reward relationship remains intact. A bond generally pays you a higher rate of interest when it has a

- **Lower credit rating:** To compensate for the higher risk of default and the higher likelihood of losing your investment
- **Longer-term maturity:** To compensate for the risk that you'll be unhappy with the bond's set interest rate if the market level of interest rates moves up

The risks you can control

In a personal finance class at the University of California, students were asked to write down what they'd like to learn. Here's what one student had to say: "I want to learn what to invest my money in now, as the stock market is overvalued and interest rates are about to go up, so bonds are dicey and banks give lousy interest — HELP!"

This student recognized the risk of price fluctuations in their investments, but they also seemed to believe, like too many people, that you actually can predict what's going to happen. How did they know that the stock market was overvalued, and why hadn't the rest of the world figured it out? How did they know that interest rates were about to go up, and why hadn't the rest of the world figured that out either?

TIP

When you invest in stocks and other growth-oriented investments, you must accept the volatility of these investments. That said, you can take several actions, which are discussed in this chapter, to greatly reduce your risk when investing in these higher-potential-return investments. Invest the money that you've earmarked for the longer term in these vehicles. Minimize the risk of these investments through diversification. Don't buy just one or two stocks; buy a number of different stocks. Later in this chapter, you find out what you need to know about diversification.

Low-risk, high-return investments

Despite what professors teach in the nation's leading business and finance graduate school programs, low-risk investments that almost certainly lead to high returns are available. Here are four such investments:

- **Paying off consumer debt:** If you're paying 10 percent, 14 percent, 18 percent, or higher interest on an outstanding credit card debt or other consumer loan, pay it off before investing. To get a comparable return through other investment vehicles (after the government takes its share of your profits), you'd have to start a new career as a loan shark. If, between federal and provincial taxes, you're in a 30 percent combined income tax bracket and you're paying 14 percent interest on consumer debt, you need to annually earn a whopping pretax return of 20 percent on your investments to justify not paying off the debt. Good luck with that.

  When your only source of funds for paying off debt is a small emergency reserve equal to a few months' living expenses, paying off your debt may involve some risk. Tap into your emergency reserves only if you have a backup source — for example, the ability to borrow from a willing family member or against a retirement account balance.

- **Investing in your health:** Eat healthy, exercise, and relax.
- **Investing in friends and family:** Invest time and effort in improving your relationships with loved ones.
- **Investing in personal and career development:** Pick up a new hobby or reinvigorate your interest in an old one, improve your communication skills, or read widely. Take a continuing education course or go back to school for a degree. Your investment will most likely lead to greater happiness and perhaps even higher paycheques.

Investment Diversification

Diversification is one of the most powerful investment concepts. It refers to saving your eggs (or investments) in different baskets. Diversification requires you to place your money in different investments with returns that are not completely correlated, which is a fancy way of saying that when some of your investments are down in value, odds are that others are up in value.

To decrease the chances of all your investments getting clobbered at the same time, you must put your money in different types of investments, such as bonds, stocks, real estate, and small business. You can further diversify your investments by investing in domestic as well as international markets.

Within a given class of investments, such as stocks, investing in different types of that class (such as different types of stocks) that perform well under various economic conditions is important. For this reason, *mutual funds,* which are diversified portfolios of securities such as stocks or bonds, are a highly useful investment vehicle. The same is true of exchange-traded funds (ETFs). ETFs are similar to mutual funds, but trade on a stock exchange. When you buy into a mutual fund or ETF, your money is pooled with the money of many other people and invested in a vast array of stocks or bonds.

TIP You can look at the benefits of diversification in two ways:

- **Diversification reduces the volatility in the value of your whole portfolio.** In other words, your portfolio can achieve the same rate of return that a single investment can provide with less fluctuation in value.
- **Diversification allows you to obtain a higher rate of return for a given level of risk.**

Keep in mind that no one, no matter whom they work for or what credentials they have, can guarantee returns on an investment. You can do good research and get lucky, but no one is free from the risk of losing money. Diversification allows you to hedge the risk of your investments.

Recent decades have shown fluctuations. In the 1990s, stocks appreciated greatly, and bonds did pretty well, too, while gold and silver did poorly. In the 2000s, stocks treaded water (except those in emerging markets), while bonds and precious metals did well. Since the end of the severe recession in 2009, stocks have soared while precious metals have greatly lagged. Because the future can't be predicted, diversifying your money in different investments is safer.

Asset allocation

Asset allocation refers to how you spread your investing dollars among different investment options (stocks, bonds, money market accounts, and so on). Before you can intelligently decide how to allocate your assets, you need to ponder a number of issues, including your present financial situation, your goals and priorities, and the pros and cons of various investment options.

Although stocks and real estate offer attractive long-term returns, they can sometimes suffer significant declines. Thus, these investments are not suitable for money that you think you may want or need to use within, say, the next five years.

TIP

Everyone should have a reserve of money — about three to six months' worth of living expenses — that's accessible in an emergency. (Refer to Chapter 2 for more on emergency reserves.)

The best place to keep money that you expect to use soon is inside a Tax-Free Savings Account (TFSA), which came into being in 2009. The name is unfortunately misleading — you could easily make the costly mistake of assuming that you can only have cash in your TFSA, just like you would in a regular bank savings or chequing account. In fact, you can hold any investment that's eligible for a Registered Retirement Savings Plan (RRSP) inside a TFSA. This includes stocks, bonds, mutual funds, ETFs, annuities, and real estate investment trusts.

Given that you plan on withdrawing the money in the near future, don't put it into stocks or other investments that can and do take regular drops in value. Your best bet is a high-interest account, money market fund, or short-term bond fund.

When you put money into a TFSA, you don't get a tax deduction. But like an RRSP, any gains on the money inside your TFSA can grow and compound tax-free. What's more, unlike withdrawals from an RRSP, which are taxed, there is no tax due on withdrawals from a TFSA. This includes not only your original contributions, but also any profits you've made.

In 2022, the maximum you could put into a TFSA for the year was capped at $6,000. This maximum is indexed to inflation and is rounded off to the nearest $500. And there's more good news: If you don't contribute the maximum in any given year, that unused amount is carried forward and added to the amount you're allowed to contribute the next year.

Money allocation for the long term

Investing money for retirement is a classic long-term goal that most people have. Your current age and the number of years until you retire are the biggest factors to consider when allocating money for long-term purposes. The younger you are and the more years you have before retirement, the more comfortable you can afford to be with growth-oriented (and more volatile) investments, such as stocks and real estate.

TIP

One useful guideline for dividing or allocating your money between longer-term growth investments, such as stocks, and more-conservative lending investments, such as bonds, is to subtract your age from 110 (120 if you want to be aggressive; 100 to be more conservative) and invest the resulting percentage in stocks. You then invest the remaining amount in bonds. For example, if you're 30 years old, you invest from 70 percent (100 – 30) to 90 percent (120 – 30) in stocks. You invest the remaining 10 percent to 30 percent in bonds.

Table 6-4 lists some guidelines for allocating long-term money based on your age and the level of risk you desire.

Your Investment Attitude	Bond Allocation (%)	Stock Allocation (%)
Play it safer	Your age	100 – your age
Middle-of-the-road	Your age – 10	110 – your age
Aggressive	Your age – 20	120 – your age

Table 6-4: *Allocating Long-Term Money*

For example, if you're the conservative sort who doesn't like a lot of risk but recognizes the value of striving for some growth and making your money work harder, you're a middle-of-the-road type. Using Table 6-4, if you're 40 years old, you may consider putting 30 percent (40 – 10) in bonds and 70 percent (110 – 40) in stocks.

In most employer retirement plans, mutual funds are the typical investment vehicle. If your employer's retirement plan includes more than one stock mutual fund as an option, you may want to try discerning which options are best. In the event that all your retirement plan's stock fund options are good, you can simply divide your stock allocation among the choices.

TIP

When one or more of the choices is an international stock fund, consider allocating a percentage of your stock fund money to overseas investments — at least 20 percent for play-it-safe investors, 25 percent to

35 percent for middle-of-the-road investors, and as much as 35 percent to 50 percent for aggressive investors.

If the 40-year-old middle-of-the-roader from the previous example is investing 70 percent in stocks, about 25 percent to 35 percent of the stock fund investments (which works out to be about 18 percent to 24 percent of the total) can be invested in a combination of U.S. and international stock funds.

In generations past, most employees didn't have to make their own investing decisions with their retirement money. That's because pension plans in which the company directs the investments were much more common. It's interesting to note that in a typical pension plan, companies choose to allocate the majority of money to stocks (about 60 percent), with a bit less placed in bonds (about 35 percent) and other investments.

Don't trade

Your goals and desire to take risk should drive the allocation of your investment dollars. As you get older, gradually scaling back on the riskiness (and, therefore, growth potential and volatility) of your portfolio generally makes sense.

Don't tinker with your portfolio daily, weekly, monthly, or even annually. (Every two to three years or so, you may want to rebalance your holdings to get your mix to a desired asset allocation, as discussed in the preceding section.) Don't engage in trading with the hopes of buying into a hot investment and selling your losers. Jumping onto a "winner" and dumping a "loser" may provide some short-term psychological comfort, but in the long term, such an investment strategy often produces below-average returns.

TIP

When an investment gets front-page coverage and everyone is talking about its stunning rise, it's definitely time to take a reality check. The higher an investment's price rises, the greater the danger that it's overpriced. Its next move may be downward. Don't follow the herd.

During the late 1990s, many technology (especially Internet) stocks had spectacular rises and attracted a huge amount of attention. However, the fact that the economy was increasingly becoming technology-based didn't mean that any price you paid for a technology stock was fine. Some investors who neglected to do basic research and bought into the attention-grabbing, high-flying technology stocks lost 80 percent to 90 percent or more of their investments in the early 2000s. Ouch!

Conversely, when things look bleak (as when stocks in general suffered significant losses in the early 2000s and then again in the late 2000s), giving up hope is easy — who wants to be associated with a loser? The more the markets fall, it seems, the more people become fearful that further drops are imminent.

However, the opposite is typically what happens: The market rebounds, often offering patient investors double-digit returns in the year or two following a large sell-off. But investors who forget about their overall asset allocation plan and panic and sell *after* a major decline miss out on what turn out to be tremendous buying opportunities.

Many people like buying everything from clothing to cars to ketchup on sale — yet whenever the stock market has a clearance sale, most investors stampede for the exits instead of snatching up great buys. Demonstrate your courage; don't follow the herd.

Investment Firms

Thousands of firms sell investments and manage money. Banks, mutual fund companies, securities brokerage firms, and even insurance companies all vie for your dollars.

Just to make matters more complicated, each industry plays in the others' backyards. You can find mutual fund companies that offer securities brokerage, insurance firms that are in the mutual fund business, and mutual fund companies that offer bank-like accounts and services. You may benefit from this competition and one-stop shopping convenience. On the other hand, some firms are novices at particular businesses and count on folks shopping by brand-name recognition.

TIP Make sure you do business with a firm that

- **Offers the best value investments in comparison to its competitors:** *Value* is the combination of performance (including service) and cost. Given the level of risk that you're comfortable with, you want investments that offer higher rates of return, but you don't want to have to pay a small fortune for them. Commissions, management fees, maintenance fees, and other charges can turn a high-performance investment into a mediocre or poor one.
- **Employs representatives who don't have an inherent self-interest in steering you into a particular type of investment:** This criterion has nothing to do with whether an investment firm hires polite, well-educated, or well-dressed people. The most important factor is the way the company compensates its employees. If the investment firm's personnel are paid on commission, be wary. Give preference to investing firms that don't tempt their employees to push one investment over another in order to generate more fees.

No-load (commission-free) mutual fund companies

Mutual funds are an ideal investment vehicle for most investors. *No-load mutual fund companies* are firms through which you can invest in mutual funds without paying sales commissions. In other words, every dollar you invest goes to work in the mutual funds you choose — nothing is siphoned off to pay sales commissions. Many of these firms also offer ETFs, which are similar to mutual funds in many ways, are (in the best cases) lower cost, and trade on a major stock exchange and, thus, can be bought and sold during the trading day.

Discount brokers

In one of the most beneficial changes for investors in the past century, the U.S. Securities and Exchange Commission (SEC) deregulated the retail brokerage industry on May 1, 1975. (In 1983, the Toronto and Montreal stock exchanges followed suit.) Prior to this date, investors were charged fixed commissions when they bought or sold stocks, bonds, and other securities. In other words, no matter which brokerage firm an investor did business with, the cost of the firm's services was set (and the level of commissions was high). After deregulation, brokerage firms could charge people whatever their little hearts desired.

Competition inevitably resulted in more and better choices. Many new brokerage firms (that didn't do business the old way) opened. They were dubbed *discount brokers* because the fees they charged customers were substantially lower than what brokers charged under the old fixed-fee system.

Even more important than saving customers money, discount brokers established a vastly improved compensation system that greatly reduced conflicts of interest. Discount brokers generally pay the salaries of their brokers. The term *discount broker* is actually not an enlightening one. Certainly, this new breed of brokerage firm saves you lots of money when you invest; you can easily save 50 percent to 80 percent through the major discount brokers. But these firms' investments are not "on sale" or "second rate." Discount brokers are simply brokers without major conflicts of interest. Of course, like any other for-profit enterprise, they're in business to make money, but they're much less likely to steer you in the wrong direction for their own benefit.

TIP

Be wary of discount brokers selling load mutual funds.

What to do when you're fleeced by any broker

You can't sue a broker just because you lose money on that person's investment recommendations. However, if you've been the victim of one of the following cardinal financial sins, you may have some legal recourse:

- **Misrepresentation and omission:** If you were told, for example, that a particular investment guaranteed returns of 15 percent per year and then the investment ended up plunging in value by 50 percent, you were misled. Misrepresentation can also be charged if you're sold an investment with hefty commissions after you were originally told that it was commission-free.

- **Unsuitable investments:** Retirees who need access to their capital are often advised to invest in limited partnerships (LPs) for safe, high yields. The yields on most LPs end up being anything but safe. LP investors have also discovered how *illiquid* (not readily converted into cash) their investments are — some can't be liquidated for up to ten years or more.
- **Churning:** If your broker is constantly trading your investments, odds are that their weekly commission cheque is getting boosted at your expense.
- **Rogue elephant salespeople:** When your broker buys or sells without your approval or ignores your request to make a change, you may be able to collect for losses caused by these actions.

TIP

Two major types of practitioners — securities lawyers and arbitration consultants — stand ready to help you recover your lost money. You can find securities lawyers by searching for *securities lawyers* online or calling your local bar association for referrals. Arbitration consultants can be found in phone directories under *arbitrators.* If you come up dry, try contacting business writers at a major newspaper in your area or at your favourite personal finance magazine. These sources may be able to give you names and numbers of folks they know.

Many such lawyers and consultants work on a *contingency fee* basis — they get a percentage (about 20 percent to 40 percent) of the amount collected. They also often ask for an up-front fee, ranging from several hundred to several thousand dollars, to help them cover their expenses and time. If they take your case and lose, they generally keep the up-front money. Securities lawyers are usually a more expensive option.

You may want to go to *arbitration* — in fact, you likely agreed to do just that (probably without realizing it) when you set up an account to work with the broker. Arbitration is usually much quicker, cheaper, and easier than going to court. You can even choose to represent yourself. The arbitrators then make a determination that neither side can squabble over or appeal.

If you decide to prepare for arbitration by yourself, the nonprofit American Arbitration Association can send you a package of background materials to help with your case. Contact the association's headquarters (800-778-7879; www.adr.org). The website is for Americans, but it offers a lot of useful general information and tips about arbitration. Although similar Canadian organizations exist, they're largely professional development bodies.

7

The Three Laws of Buying Insurance

Unless you work in the industry, you may find insurance to be a dreadfully boring topic. Most people associate insurance with disease, death, and disaster and would rather do just about anything other than review their policies or spend money on insurance. But because you won't want to deal with money hassles when you're coping with catastrophes — illness, disability, death, fires, floods, earthquakes, and so on — you should secure insurance well *before* you need it.

Insurance is probably the most misunderstood and least monitored area of personal finance. Studies by the U.S. nonprofit National Insurance Consumer Organization show that about 90 percent of people purchase and carry the wrong types and amounts of insurance coverage. Most people are overwhelmed by all the jargon in sales and policy statements. Thus, they pay more than necessary for their policies and get coverage they don't really need while failing to obtain coverage that they really should have.

Your patience and interest in finding out about insurance is surely limited, so this chapter boils down the subject to three fairly simple but powerful concepts that can easily save you big bucks:

- Insure for the big stuff; don't sweat the small stuff.
- Buy broad coverage.
- Shop around and buy direct.

And while you're saving money, you can still get the quality coverage you need to avoid a financial catastrophe.

Insure for the Big Stuff; Don't Sweat the Small Stuff

What if you could buy insurance that would pay for the cost of a restaurant meal if you got food poisoning? Even if you were splurging at a fancy restaurant, you wouldn't have a lot of money at stake, so you'd probably decline that coverage.

The point of insurance is to protect against losses that would be financially catastrophic to you, not to smooth out the bumps of everyday life. The preceding example about restaurant insurance is silly, but some people buy equally foolish policies without knowing it.

The following sections tell you how to get the most appropriate insurance coverage for your money. They start off with the "biggies" that are worth your money, and then they work down to some insurance options that are less worthy of your dollars.

Buy insurance to cover financial catastrophes

TIP

You want to insure against what could be a huge financial loss for you or your dependants. The price of insurance isn't cheap, but it's relatively small in comparison to the potential total loss from a financial catastrophe.

The beauty of insurance is that it spreads risks over millions of other people. If your home were to burn to the ground, paying the rebuilding cost out of your own pocket probably would be a financial catastrophe. If you have insurance, the premiums paid by you and all the other homeowners collectively can easily pay the bills.

Think for a moment about what your most valuable assets are. Also consider potential large expenses. Perhaps they include the following:

- **Future income:** During your working years, your most valuable asset is probably your future earnings. If you were disabled and unable to work, what would you live on? Long-term disability insurance exists to help you handle this type of situation. If you have a family that's financially dependent on your earnings, how would your family manage if you died? Life insurance can fill the monetary void left by your death.
- **Business:** If you're a business owner, what would happen if you were sued for hundreds of thousands of dollars or a million dollars or more for negligence in some work that you messed up? Liability insurance can protect you.
- **Health:** In this age of soaring medical costs, you can easily rack up significant bills in short order. Depending on your situation, it may pay to buy extended medical health insurance coverage that covers you for expenses your provincial plan doesn't, such as prescription drugs, dental care, physical therapists, and counselling.

Psychologically, buying insurance coverage for the little things that are more likely to occur is tempting. You don't want to feel like you're wasting your insurance dollars. You want to get some of your money back, darn it! You're more *likely* to get into a fender bender with your car or have a package lost in the mail than you are to lose your home to fire or suffer a long-term disability. But if the fender bender costs $500 (which you end up paying out of your pocket because you took a high deductible; see the next section) or the post office loses your package worth $50 or $100, you won't be facing a financial disaster.

On the other hand, if you lose your ability to earn an income because of a disability, or if you're sued for $1 million and you're not insured against such catastrophes, not only will you be extremely unhappy, but you may also face financial ruin. Some people rationalize, "Yes, but what are the odds that I'll suffer a long-term disability or that I'll be sued for $1 million?" Yes, the odds are quite low, but the risk is there. The problem is that you just don't know what, or when, bad luck may befall you.

And don't make the mistake of thinking that you can figure the odds better than the insurance companies can. The insurance companies predict the probability of your making a claim, large or small, with a great deal of accuracy. They employ armies of number-crunching actuaries to calculate the odds that bad things will happen and the frequency of current policyholders' making particular types of claims. The companies then price their policies accordingly.

So, buying (or not buying) insurance based on your perception of the likelihood of needing the coverage is foolish. Insurance companies aren't stupid; in fact, they're ruthlessly smart. When insurance companies price policies, they look at several factors to determine the likelihood of your filing a claim. Take the example of auto insurance. Who do you think will pay more for auto insurance: A single 20-year-old male who lives the fast life in a city known for car thefts, drives a turbo sports car, and has received two speeding tickets in the past year? Or a couple in their 40s, living in an area where car thefts are rare, driving a four-door sedan, with clean driving records?

Take the highest deductible you can afford

Most insurance policies have *deductibles* — the maximum amount you must pay in the event of a loss before your insurance coverage kicks in and begins paying out. On many policies, such as auto and homeowner's or renter's coverage, many folks opt for a $100 to $250 deductible.

Here are some benefits of taking a higher deductible:

- **You save premium dollars.** Year in and year out, you can enjoy the lower cost of an insurance policy with a high deductible. You may be able to shave 15 percent to 20 percent off the cost of your policy. Suppose, for example, that you can reduce the cost of your policy by $150 per year by raising your deductible from $250 to $1,000. That $750 worth of coverage is costing you $150 per year. So, you'd need to have a claim of $1,000 or more every five years — highly unlikely — to come out ahead. If you're that accident-prone, guess what? The insurance company will raise your premiums.

- **You don't have the hassles of filing small claims.** If you have a $300 loss on a policy with a $100 deductible, you need to file a claim to get your $200 (the amount you're covered for after your deductible). Filing an insurance claim can be an aggravating experience that takes hours. In some cases, you may even have your claim denied after jumping through all the necessary hoops. Getting your due may require prolonged haggling.

When you have low deductibles, you may file more claims (although this doesn't necessarily mean that you'll get more money). After filing more claims, you may be "rewarded" with higher premiums — in addition to the headache you get from preparing all those blasted forms! Filing more claims may even cause cancellation of your coverage.

Avoid small-potato policies

A good insurance policy can seem expensive. A policy that doesn't cost much, on the other hand, can fool you into thinking that you're getting something for next to nothing. Policies that cost little also cover little — they're priced low because they don't cover large potential losses.

Following are examples of common "small-potato" insurance policies that are generally a waste of your hard-earned dollars. As you read through this list, you may find examples of policies that you bought and that you feel paid for themselves. You may be saying, "But I collected on that policy you're telling me not to buy!" Sure, getting "reimbursed" for the hassle of having something go wrong is comforting. But consider all such policies that you bought or may buy over the course of your life. You're not going to come out ahead in the aggregate — if you did, insurance companies would lose money. These policies aren't worth the cost relative to the small potential benefit. On average, insurance companies pay out just 60 cents in benefits on every dollar collected. Many of the following policies pay back even less — around 20 cents in benefits (claims) for every insurance premium dollar spent.

Extended warranty and repair plans

Isn't it ironic that right after salespeople persuade you to buy a particular television, computer, car, or smartphone — in part by saying how reliable the product is — they try to convince you to spend more money to insure against the failure of the item? If the product is so good, why do you need such insurance?

Extended warranty and repair plans are expensive and unnecessary short-term insurance policies. Product manufacturers' warranties typically cover any problems that occur in the first year or even several years. After that, paying for a repair out of your own pocket isn't a financial catastrophe.

TIP

Some credit card issuers automatically double the manufacturer's warranty without additional charge on items purchased with their cards. However, the cards that do this typically are higher-cost premium cards, so this is no free lunch — you're paying for this protection in terms of higher fees.

Home warranty plans

A third-party new home warranty is mandatory for most buyers in Ontario and Quebec, as well as Alberta, British Columbia, and Manitoba. In other provinces (at least as of the time of writing), they're still optional. If you're buying a home in another province, and your real estate agent or the seller of a home wants to pay the cost of a home warranty plan for you, turning down the offer would be ungracious. (As Grandma would say, you shouldn't look a gift horse in the mouth.) But don't buy this type of plan for yourself unless you're required to by provincial regulations. In addition to requiring some sort of fee (around $50 to $100), home warranty plans limit how much they'll pay for problems.

Your money is best spent hiring a competent inspector to uncover problems and fix them *before* you purchase the home. If you buy a house, you should expect to spend money on repairs and maintenance; don't waste money purchasing insurance for such expenses.

Dental insurance

If your employer pays for dental insurance, you can take advantage of it. But don't pay for this coverage on your own. Dental insurance generally covers a couple of dental cleanings each year and limits payments for more expensive work.

Credit life and credit disability policies

Credit life policies pay a small benefit if you die with an outstanding loan. *Credit disability policies* pay a small monthly income in the event of a disability. Banks and their credit card divisions usually sell these policies. Some companies sell insurance to pay off your credit card bill in the event of your death or disability, or to cover minimum monthly payments for a temporary period during specified life transition events (such as loss of a job, divorce, and so on).

The cost of such insurance seems low, but that's because the potential benefits are relatively small. In fact, given what little insurance you're buying, these policies are expensive. If you need life or disability insurance, buy it. But get enough coverage, and buy it in a separate, cost-effective policy.

TIP: If you're in poor health and you can buy these insurance policies without a medical evaluation, you may be an exception to the "don't buy it" rule. In this case, these policies may be the only ones to which you have access — another reason these policies are expensive. The people in good health are paying for the people with poor health who can enroll without a medical examination and who undoubtedly file more claims.

Mail insurance

TIP: You buy a $40 gift for a friend, and when you go to the post office to ship it, the friendly postal clerk asks whether you want to insure it. For a few bucks, you think, "Why not?" Canada Post rarely loses or damages things. Go spend your money on something else — or better yet, invest it.

Cellphone insurance

It's understandable that if you just shelled out $700 or more for the latest smartphone (especially if you bought one for a teenager in your household), you'd like to protect against the loss or damage of said device. If you can't afford to replace such a costly cellphone, then don't spend that much on one in the first place. But if you insist on a costly smartphone purchase, the insurance isn't worth it. Reviews of recent plans show that the coverage will cost you $150 to $300 just for the first two years and, if you do have a loss, you'll also get whacked with a $100 to $200 deductible.

Contact lens insurance

The things that people come up with to waste money on are astounding. Contact lens insurance really does exist. The money goes to replace your contacts if you lose or tear them. Lenses are relatively inexpensive. Don't waste your money on this kind of insurance.

Little-stuff riders

Many policies that are worth buying, such as auto and disability insurance, can have all sorts of riders added on. These *riders* are extra bells and whistles that insurance agents and companies like to sell because of the high profit margin they provide (for *them*). On auto insurance policies, for example, you can buy a rider for a few bucks per year that pays you $25 each time your car needs to be towed. Having your vehicle towed isn't going to bankrupt you, so it isn't worth insuring against.

Likewise, small insurance policies that are sold as add-ons to bigger insurance policies are usually unnecessary and overpriced. For example, you can buy some disability insurance policies with a small amount of life insurance added on. If you need life insurance, purchasing it in a separate policy is less costly.

Buy Broad Coverage

Purchasing coverage that's too narrow is another major mistake people make when buying insurance. Such policies often seem like cheap ways to put your fears to rest. For example, instead of buying life insurance, some folks buy flight insurance at an airport self-service kiosk. They seem to worry more about their mortality when getting on an airplane than they do when getting into a car. If they die on the flight, their beneficiaries collect. But if they die the next day in a car accident or get some dreaded disease — which is statistically far, *far* more likely than going down in a jet — the beneficiaries get nothing from flight insurance. Buy life insurance (broad coverage to protect your loved ones financially in the event of your untimely demise no matter the cause), not flight insurance (narrow coverage).

The medical equivalent of flight insurance is cancer insurance. Older people, who are fearful of having their life savings depleted by a long battle with this dreaded disease, are easy prey for this narrow insurance. If you get cancer, cancer insurance pays the bills. But what if you get heart disease, diabetes, or some other disease? Cancer insurance won't pay these costs. Purchase major medical coverage, not cancer insurance.

Recognize fears

Fears, such as getting cancer, are natural and inescapable. Although you may not have control over the emotions that your fears invoke, you must often ignore those emotions in order to make rational insurance decisions. In other words, getting shaky in the knees and sweaty in the palms when boarding an airplane is okay, but letting your fear of flying cause you to make poor insurance decisions is not okay, especially when those decisions affect the financial security of your loved ones.

Prepare for natural disasters — insurance and otherwise

You'll find it nearly impossible to get insurance coverage that includes every possibility of catastrophe. For example, when purchasing homeowner's coverage, you may find that losses from floods and earthquakes are excluded. You may be able to secure such coverage in separate policies, which you should do if you live in an area subject to such risks. Many people don't understand these risks, and insurers don't always educate customers about such gaping holes in their policies.

TIP In addition to filling those voids, also think about and plan for the nonfinancial issues that inevitably arise in a catastrophe. For example, make sure you have

- A meeting place for you and your loved ones if you're separated during a disaster (and a friend or family member who lives outside your area to serve as a common point of contact)
- An escape plan in the event that your area is hit with flooding or some other natural disaster (tornado, hurricane, earthquake, fire, or mudslide)
- The security of having taken steps to make your home safer in the event of an earthquake or fire (for instance, securing shelving and heavy objects from falling and tipping, and installing smoke detectors and fire extinguishers)
- A plan for what you'll do for food, clothing, and shelter if your home becomes uninhabitable

You get the idea. Although you can't possibly predict what's going to happen and when, you can find out about the risks for your area. In addition to buying the broadest possible coverage, you should also make contingency plans for disasters.

Shop Around and Buy Direct

Whether you're looking at auto, home, life, disability, or other types of coverage, some companies may charge double or triple the rates that other companies charge for the same coverage. Insurers that charge the higher rates may not be better about paying claims, however. You may even end up with the worst of both possible worlds — high prices *and* lousy service.

Most insurance is sold through agents and brokers who earn commissions based on what they sell. The commissions, of course, can bias what they recommend.

Not surprisingly, policies that pay agents the biggest commissions also tend to be more costly. In fact, insurance companies compete for the attention of agents by offering bigger commissions. In publications targeted to insurance agents, there are often ads in which the largest text is the commission percentage offered to agents who sell the advertiser's products.

Besides the attraction of policies that pay higher commissions, agents also get hooked, financially speaking, on companies whose policies they sell frequently. After agents sell a certain amount of a company's insurance policies, they are rewarded with bigger commission percentages (and other perks) on any future sales. Just as airlines bribe frequent flyers with mileage bonuses, insurers bribe agents with heftier commissions and awards such as trips and costly goods.

Shopping around is a challenge not only because most insurance is sold by agents working on commission, but also because insurers set their rates in mysterious ways. Every company has a different way of analyzing how much of a risk you are; one company may offer low rates to your friend but not to you, and vicc versa.

Despite the obstacles, several strategies exist for obtaining low-cost, high-quality policies. The following sections offer smart ways to shop for insurance.

Look at employer and other group plans

When you buy insurance as part of a larger group, you generally get a lower price because of the purchasing power of the group. Most of the health and disability policies that you can access through your employer are less costly than equivalent coverage you can buy on your own.

TIP Likewise, many occupations have professional associations through which you may be able to obtain lower-cost policies. Not all associations offer better deals on insurance — compare their policy features and costs with other options.

Life insurance is an exception to the rule that states that group policies offer better value than individual policies. Group life insurance plans usually aren't cheaper than the best life insurance policies that you can buy individually. However, group policies may have the attraction of convenience (ease of enrollment and avoidance of lengthy sales pitches from life insurance salespeople). Group life insurance policies that allow you to enroll without a medical evaluation are usually more expensive, because such plans attract more people with health problems who can't get coverage on their own. If you're in good health, you should definitely shop around for life insurance.

Insurance agents who want to sell you an individual policy can come up with 101 reasons why buying from them is preferable to buying through your employer or some other group. In most cases, agents' arguments for buying an individual policy from them include self-serving hype.

One valid issue that agents raise is that if you leave your job, you'll lose your group coverage. Sometimes that may be true. For example, if you know that you're going to be leaving your job to become self-employed, securing an individual disability policy before you leave your job makes sense. However, your employer's health insurer may allow you to buy an individual policy when you leave.

In most cases, group plans, especially through an employer, offer good benefits. If the group policy is cheaper than a comparable individual policy, you'll save money overall buying through the group plan.

Buy insurance without paying sales commissions

Buying policies from the increasing number of companies that are selling their policies directly to the public without the insurance agent and the agent's commission is your best bet for getting a good insurance value. Just as you can purchase no-load mutual funds directly from an investment company without paying any sales commission, you also can buy no-load insurance.

Annuities, investment/insurance products traditionally sold through insurance agents, are also now available directly to the customer, without commission.

About the Authors

Tony Martin has always had an innate understanding of money. Instead of getting his (tiny) allowance paid out to him weekly in shiny coins like his brothers did, he asked his mom to keep track of how much he was owed.

After emerging from Queen's University business school with a BCom, despite a transcript that listed courses such as "Electronic Music" and "The Philosophy of Religion," Tony set off to see the world. On his return, he joined CBC radio, and ever since, he has been helping people understand the world of money.

Noticing there was an absence of sound, easy-to-read financial guides for Canadians that were also easy to implement, Tony approached the publishers of the *For Dummies* series with the idea of writing a Canadian-centric version of *Personal Finance For Dummies.* And thus, the first non-U.S. *For Dummies* title was born, with Tony becoming the first Canadian — and first ever non-American — *For Dummies* author. In addition to coauthoring the national Canadian best-seller *Personal Finance For Canadians For Dummies,* Tony and Eric also worked together to write the best-selling *Investing For Canadians For Dummies.*

For over a decade, Tony's widely read column "Me and My Money" appeared in the *Globe and Mail*'s weekend personal finance section. He was also the investing columnist for *Report on Business Magazine.* His work has been featured in many leading publications, including *MoneySense, IE Money, Profit,*

Reader's Digest, and *Canadian Business.* Tony is a frequent commentator and speaker on personal finance and investing and regularly appears on television and radio, including BNN CBC Radio, CBC Television, BCC, and TVOntario.

Tony has been instrumental in the design and development of many leading online resources, including an interactive investor training program using simulated stock market transactions. He also was editorial head for i | money.com, Canada's first financial website, which later became the content for Canoe.ca. He has worked extensively as a communications consultant, editorial advisor, and educator. His clients include Bank of America, Barrick, BMO, Business Development Bank of Canada, Fidelity, Geico, IBM, Integra, Manulife, The Principal Group, Scotiabank, Sun Life Financial, TD Bank, and VISA Canada.

Tony is also an accomplished and engaging teacher, lecturer, and management trainer. He leads courses across the country on finance and accounting, as well as speaking and presenting, business writing, writing for the web, public speaking and presenting, negotiating, and conflict resolution for national management training leaders, as well as many major companies and organizations, including Shoppers Drug Mart, Siemens, the Ontario Government, and Ontario Power Corp.

Eric Tyson is an internationally acclaimed and best-selling personal finance author and speaker. He has worked with and taught people from all financial situations, so he knows the financial concerns and questions of real folks. Despite having an MBA from the Stanford Graduate School of Business and a BS in economics and biology from Yale University, Eric remains a master of "keeping it simple."

He figured out how to pursue his dream after working as a management consultant to Fortune 500 financial services firms. Eric took his inside knowledge of the banking, investment, and insurance industries and committed himself to making personal financial management accessible to all. He is the author of several national best-selling financial books in Wiley's *For Dummies* series, including books on personal finance, investing, mutual funds, home buying (coauthor), and real estate investing (coauthor). His *Personal Finance For Dummies* (Wiley) won the Benjamin Franklin Award for best business book of the year. An accomplished personal finance writer, his "Investors' Guide" syndicated column, distributed by King Features, is read by millions nationally, and he was an award-winning columnist for the *San Francisco Examiner*. Eric's work has been featured and quoted in hundreds of local and national publications, including *Newsweek, The Wall Street Journal, Los Angeles Times, Chicago Tribune, Forbes, Kiplinger's Personal Finance, Parenting, Money,* and *Bottom Line/Personal;* on NBC's *Today Show,* ABC, CNBC, PBS's *Nightly Business Report,* CNN, and FOX; and on CBS national radio, NPR's *Marketplace Money,* and Bloomberg Radio.

Eric's website is `www.erictyson.com`.

